Understanding Anger in the Church

UNDERSTANDING ANGER IN THE CHURCH

DANIEL G. BAGBY

BROADMAN PRESS/Nashville, Tennessee

Dewey Decimal Classification: 152.4
Subject heading: ANGER
Library of Congress Catalog Card Number: 79-52000
Printed in the United States of America.

Scripture references marked RSV are from
the Revise Standard Version of the Bible,
copyrighted 1946, 1952, © 1971, 1973.

Foreword

The "hidden curriculum" of learning what many little children recall about their church lives when they become adults is: conflict, flaring tempers, family feuds, and dinner-table rehearsals of grudges. Negative, is it not? Our usual approach to this "nitty gritty" of church life is to smile, be sweet, and speak negatively of all those negative-minded people. Such "positive thinking" is well-placed if its objective is to have done with old war stories, build a constructive view of the church, and get on with the redemptive purposes of the people of God. However, such "sweetness and light" *may* be a deliberate resolve to *exclude* the angry ones, to ignore the roots of their resistance, and to consider them as something considerably less than persons. They *are* made in the image of God, people for whom Christ died. Their anger and resentment are really shrieks of pain upon having been severely mistreated, neglected, ignored, excluded, and denigrated.

For the first time of which I am aware, Daniel Bagby's book, which you are about to have the time of your life reading, is an eyewitness report of the driving forces behind the alienation of church members. He bases his work on solid interviewing of nearly a hundred such alienated church members and upon his intensive experience as a chaplain, as an associate pastor, and as a seasoned senior pastor. This is no armchair speculative guess work. This is not just some wise person's expert opinion. It is tested research.

Yet, it is written in the most forthright pastor-to-you language. You are not burdened down with the buckets and ringing bells of somebody's "laboratory mice approach" to things. He speaks as a "teacher come from God" to the person who has had his or her spiritual life fall to pieces in chaos. He speaks of God who created a universe in which, nevertheless, *accidents* do happen for which *no* blame can be assigned. "God steps into each of these events to make good out of evil." He has a wholesome respect for the perdurance of original sin in the pretensions of perfection of my and your piety. He is at work throughout the book pointing to the power of forgiveness, the repetitive necessity of forgiveness, and the intervention of the Holy Spirit.

Daniel Bagby does not write as a summertime patriot of the *koinonia* of the Christian fellowship. He writes as a soldier of the cross who is there at the difficult business meeting, at the collision of two or more families over their vested interests in the church, at the quiet desperation of the divorced parent who feels the church is not interested in his or her children anymore, and of the retired person whose "full time" attention to the church is rebuffed. The lay person should put this book at the top of his or her "must" reading list. The pastor who is not asleep at the wheel will stop at the nearest book store, get the book, and read it at one sitting. Otherwise, his congregation will be telling him about how necessary it is that he "be angry and sin not." I commend this book to Christians and non-Christians alike. It tells us what it really means to come to the Lord Jesus Christ "just as we are without one plea."

WAYNE E. OATES, Th.D.
Professor of Psychiatry and Behavioral Sciences
Director, Program in Ethics and Pastoral Counseling
University of Louisville School of Medicine

Contents

Introduction

The service had been in progress only ten minutes when one of the ushers quietly slipped a note to the senior pastor: "Deacon Moore is out in the hall and is threatening to stay out of worship as long as the assistant pastor is in the service." As the minister made his way to this church leader's presence, two other members passed by him disturbed that any deacon should act so strongly.

A business session is in progress, with entrenched sides making stronger and stronger remarks to each other about their opinions and their worth. One man, seated up front, begins to breathe heavily, stands up suddenly, and tells the last speaker and several resisting the motion under consideration that their "prejudice has been the main obstacle" in their acceptance of the recommendation. As the one addressed begins to stand and respond (somewhat shaken), a third man in the back who has been shaking his head for quite some time, picks up his coat, stands up abruptly, pushes his way down a row, and storms out of the meeting without a comment.

She and her children have been absent from Bible study (Sunday School) for almost two months, and as she awkwardly searches for her daughter's classroom she is met in the hall by the child's teacher who looks surprised that the girl's name is not on the roll. The teacher then proceeds to explain about the art project the class is doing and how everyone needs to come weekly and work on it in the classroom. The mother's eyes gleam; she quickly leads her children out the door and into the car, with a sealed promise that she and hers will never come to Bible study in that church again.

"Why did I quit going to that church? I'll tell you why! You see this picture? That's my boy, and today he's doing fine, living somewhere else and in school—fine grades. But there was a time when he wasn't doing so well. I had been divorced for three years when Tommy started getting into trouble, stealing bicycles. I knew I could give him some help, but I knew he needed a father figure, too. He just adored our pastor, and I called him, and I said to him, 'Brother Cox, my son's in trouble, and I really need your help.' I explained the situation to him, and he promised me he'd come out to talk to Tommy—he never did. I called three times, and each time he was going to get out here. He never came. My son finally got into trouble and had to go to the detention center. I could have used some help then, but no one asked me anything—or came by. I've never been there since—and you're the first pastor who has come here to visit me since then—nine years ago."

John Erskine, boys' Sunday School teacher for over twenty years, is suddenly taken to the hospital quite ill. The Youth minister drops in to see him directly after a difficult operation; John comments how his greatest pain is not being able to be with "his boys on Sunday." The pastor suggests that he not worry about that since his class has been given to another teacher. John recovers physically . . . but quietly starts attending another congregation.

A friend of the treasurer calls to tell him that Mrs. Hoffman, another member of the church, was deeply offended by his curt reply to her one day in the narthex. The treasurer calls the member, only to be told it is no matter of concern and that she cannot imagine what their mutual friend was referring to and coolly terminates the conversation.

Unusual happenings? Rare behavior? Only to those who have missed the many shades and shapes of anger among sincere but often awkward believers who struggle with the stewardship of their exasperation. The resultant feelings often lead to alienation from church friends, separation from the fellowship, and/or broken relationships and unhealed pain.

What is the answer? At least one answer is a better understanding of each particular situation. A better understanding of anger among church members must at least include a search for better approaches to the appropriate expression and manifestation of anger, disappointment, and irritation among the saints.

This book is written with pastor, deacon, and concerned Christian citizen in mind—in that order. My experience with the church and with its membership is that one major problem in the body is a proper understanding of how anger occurs in the local congregation, how it is expressed, and how it may effectively and responsibly be channeled in the Christian community. I am a pastor with over ten years of "in the trenches" experience in dealing with the local church and its members. My first interest in the alienated church member began as a chaplain to juvenile offenders in the heart of Louisville. I heard so many stories of disappointment and anger with the church that I decided to become a student of the problem and try to find some answers. My keen interest took new shape as I became associate pastor of Ravensworth Baptist Church in Annandale, Virginia, and noticed how many church members on the roll were never around. I asked the deacons and senior pastor for permission to select twelve families whom they knew to be disgruntled disappointed, or disturbed with the church and to consult with me as I tried to visit with these people and minister to them. My concern was to discover how families and church members become so alienated from the church—and what can be done about it. I was so impressed with what I learned that in returning to the seminary I chose to spend research time on my doctorate in a careful plan to interview and learn from forty inactive and annoyed church families. What I learned from them became a personal plan of ministry I adopted in my next congregation, Calvary Baptist Church of West Lafayette, Indiana. The joy of witnessing reconciliation, participating in deepened Christian understanding, and seeing people released from destructive church relationships into creative Christian freedom has led me to offer what I have learned (and continue to learn) from others. I hope these pages will aid you in ministry and Christian stewardship in your congregation.

The plan in the next few pages is to suggest some of the different forms and shapes of anger, disappointment, and irritation in the church to examine the minister's own stewardship of anger as influential in the healing of anger, and then to deal with each distinct aspect of anger. The primary emphasis will be on how to handle, direct, and constructively channel each manifestation. Concluding chapters assess the church's redemptive function with anger in the small-group setting in the context of the gathered community (in worship), and with regard to preventive measures which either anticipate or properly channel unnecessary differences among the body of believers.

May God use this material toward reconciliation and redemption in his community!

1

The Many Shades and Shapes of Anger

The body of Christ has always had trouble trying to express strong emotions appropriately. Early Christians in Galatia (Gal. 1:7), Corinth (2 Cor. 10:2), and elsewhere (Eph. 4:26,31) struggled with deep feelings and differences which often became destructive and caused divisions in the young fellowships. Conflict and anger were often ignored until major problems developed, and the painful consequences of unexamined and unchecked feelings frequently brought about unnecessary suspicion and isolation among church members.

Were such clashes and conflicts unavoidable, or did they result from a poor management of God's gift of feelings? A careful study of Scripture will, I believe, reveal not only that such alienation was frequently unnecessary but was also the direct result of poorly channeled comments and actions. The Spirit of God has always been willing to harmonize relationships. But the constant temptation of believers (then and now) was not to rely on the mediating power of God but to react hastily in a given situation and, in the process, adopt old and inadequate patterns from a world that had little but destructive models for conflict resolution. Nor was the problem only one of inappropriate feelings; a second major struggle for Christians was one of finding constructive channels ᶠor

17

very appropriate strong feelings—that by virtue of unsuitable choice in the *manner* of expression went either ignored, rejected, or condemned. Paul devoted much energy and time to "putting out the brushfires" of Christian controversy; he served as admonisher, clarifier, interpreter, and peacemaker in many circumstances. The early church from time to time relied on "mediators" who would bring the Spirit of Christ's peace to bear on otherwise unbearable dissension.

This book is designed to offer one such *peacemaker* model for the modern church of Jesus Christ. In a time where division, isolation, and misunderstanding continue to plague the message of the gospel, it is my hope that all unnecessary alienation and division in the church be minimized. One helpful approach which I have found in reducing intra-church clashes is contained in this three-part peacemaker helper. I will propose three steps in approaching anger, isolation, and dissension in the church: (1) identification of the issues and/or feelings involved in a given situation; (2) the development of some constructive channels and ways to communicate these feelings appropriately within the local church; and (3) the acceptance of a spiritual atmosphere and communion that will allow for differences and strong feelings to coexist (spiritual detente?) amicably.

There is obviously not enough room or time to discuss all feelings and emotions at work in the fellowship of believers. Our comments must of necessity be limited to a discussion of the proper stewardship and management of anger. I choose to devote attention primarily to anger because my experience with anger leads me to believe that it is the least understood of the strong emotions which affect Christians in the world. Anger has, in fact, been so quickly condemned in Christian circles that three very important misunderstandings with regard to this "queen of the passions" have occurred: (1) there is an unfortunate impression that all anger is bad and, therefore, sinful; (2) such an impression has led well-meaning Christians to quietly ignore anger as a significant emotion, often disguising its occurrence and mishandling its manifestation; (3) a persistent illusion exists that negative feelings, if ignored, will not continue to influence and affect future relationships.

Each of the above misunderstandings have led to a great deal of unhappiness in the local church. The disguise and rejection of anger has given birth to many shades and shapes of misunderstood experiences. The lonely and painful consequences of unattended anger have often created disunity and awkwardness in fellowships. Perhaps a few examples of the most common difficulties which anger evokes will most clearly describe the poor stewardship of anger in the church.

The Angry/Depressed

As a pastoral counselor, I am frequently approached by persons in the church who are experiencing irregular and surprising moments of depression. They describe a daily life which contains all the ingredients necessary for happiness, and yet they display a certain "poverty of attitude" which unexpectedly controls their outlook at a given moment. They are seized by unexcitement, inertia, and depression. As I begin to explore various areas of concern with them, I detect mixed feelings with regard to certain close relationships. Before long we are centering on a particular person or event that has aroused deep feelings of resentment in them.

Such persons resist, at first, any suggestions that they might be experiencing anger or resentment. They have learned early to submerge controversial and negative feelings. Such individuals have also frequently found that to acknowledge or express their feelings has been very unrewarding. Conditioned to ignore anger toward others as isolating and painful, they find it far more bearable to internalize these strong emotions. Depression is very often a consequence of "swallowed" anger that has never been acknowledged.

Many committed Christians have been taught all their lives that anger should never show. They are schooled in the popular procedure of turning anger inside rather than "letting it out," and they suffer first from the effects of feeling "bad" (depressed) and second from the burden of carrying unexplored feelings. It is a great deal more acceptable in our society to be depressed than angry. Hence the unnatural but prevailing shape of anger is an unfocused, draining, and often paralyzing dejection. Left with the choice of hurting themselves or others, these conscientious people choose to hurt themselves—and yet only rarely recognize the source of their pain or the extent of the internal damage they accept for themselves.

The Angry/Outspoken

Unlike those who struggle to release strong feelings, some people own the gift and burden of emotional directness. They have been trained to be candid, honest, and open about how they feel. When experiencing anger or resentment, these persons, unlike those who swallow feelings, do exactly the reverse; they are very outspoken, often stating their deep feelings to the first person who chances to be available. They have the gift of open confrontation; they frequently lack a sense of timing in their expression of anger and often have difficulty controlling the intensity of their feelings in conveying them to someone else.

Such persons will usually not experience depression but far more likely will encounter isolation and loneliness because few people know exactly how to handle uninhibited feelings as expressed so immediately and directly by some people. The shape of anger in these "sons of thunder" contains the gift of clarity and honest openness (there is no deception in the conversation!). The main difficulty in this approach to communicating anger is that it requires a maturity on the receiver's part that is too often assumed and too seldom present.

Another influence at work in this particular use of anger is sometimes the threat of intimacy perceived between individuals. Some persons use verbal expressions of anger as a tool to gain distance or "space" in a relationship. Every individual possesses different needs for closeness in a fellowship of persons. When that boundary line of privacy is invaded, such an individual may use intense feelings to thwart further attempts at closeness not desired. As a pastor I am often made aware of expressions of deep feelings by parishioners whose main goal is not so much to "tell someone off" as to create some needed distance in a relationship that is becoming strained and uncomfortable by a sense of what I would call premature intimacy.

Perhaps of all the known shapes of anger, the one most feared by Christians is the outspoken expression of deep feelings. The fear of being overwhelmed by such intense emotions governs the avoidance of such openly expressed feelings in a congregation.

The Angry/Afraid

There is another dimension to anger, conditioned largely by a culture that accepts fear far more readily than "being mad." Some people in the Christian fellowship at times go through experiences of fear and general anxiety about certain changes or events in their lives that in and of themselves would not produce such dread.

Church members, who are otherwise the backbone of the church in service, will at times draw back and experience enough fear in their lives that they begin to feel paralyzed and unable to take on responsibilities. The initial fears over actions and feelings they do not understand is compounded by the additional fear of helplessness at reversing the awful panic that at times grips them in a draining hold.

This shape of anger produces a withdrawal in itself, for persons under the influence of such fears sense themselves uncomfortable around others. They dread the possibility of being overcome by this unspecified anxiety and of being neither able to explain themselves to friends nor to avoid the embarrassment of their "silly" behavior (as they see it).

Christians who are heavily dependent on the approval of others are often plagued by such fears. Underlying this fright is a dimension of deep resentment that they are, in fact, so deeply servant to the opinions of other people. Very often this sense of fear carries over to their relationship with God, whom they perceive as judging them—

not so much (at first glance) for their inability to move beyond their fears—as for their underlying anger toward him for not rescuing them from their plight. To admit such anger at God would be for them to fly against all that they have been taught concerning him and themselves (for they have probably grown up in the distorted atmosphere which implies that God never forgives anger and that Christians never get angry). It is, again, far more acceptable in this instance to be afraid of God than to be angry with him when in actuality, the latter is to take him more seriously than the former.

The Angry/Numb

The severity of stored-up angry feelings will occasionally produce an "anesthesia of feelings" which mistakenly is perceived by the membership at large as apathy. What church members frequently describe as "unconcerned" and "inactive" members in a local congregation may actually be a group of persons whose extended experience of deep resentment has gone ignored or unnoticed for a period of time. Some people patiently grieve through smoldering, angry reactions in the hope that one day someone will take notice and hear their struggle. When time and fatigue eventually suggest that their hope of detection is in vain (for they do want their feelings detected and recognized), they settle for the opposite of what they wanted: They trade a caring quality of indignation for a thick overcoat of anesthesia. The new shade of apathy is designed to protect them from caring so much that they continue to suffer. They never quit caring; they just innoculate themselves from its intensity in order to survive in or outside the church.

Such caring members soon begin to pull away from what had been a heavy involvement in the church to a position of distance and quiet indignation. They care enough for the fellowship that they decide not to expose it to the pain and alienation they themselves are in; they would rather fade out than cause more dissension in the body. They must be given credit for not wishing to pull anyone down in their resentment, but the quiet kind of damage which they accept in exchange for their silent absence is an even dearer price to be paid by them and by the fellowship. Walls are here permanently erected between what once were solid friendships; isolation is established where there was once genuine communion. Anger's shape becomes destructive in this case first because its presence has gone unnoticed and secondly because its disguise places it out of recognition for healing.

There is a distinction to be made at this point between transitional anger and unresolved resentment that takes the shape of numbness. A normal experience in the process of grieving the loss of a loved one is often marked by a temporary numbness of feeling that is God's way of protecting an individual from the full force of his emotions during difficult times. Such a therapeutic anesthetic is not to be confused with the adoption of a stance of apathy toward the church, issues, and persons on the face of ongoing lack of attention to deep feelings. A church member who feels ignored or slighted over and over again may eventually decide that he will never care to the point that being ignored will hurt. Yet the emotions and the alienation do not disappear; they stand slightly "dressed up" in shades of inactivity and cautious, cool removal from the scene.

Color these persons numb but not uncaring. They care so much, in fact, that they must develop a protective layer over their emotions in order to function around the fellowship. Their tragedy, and that of the body of Christ to which they belong, is that vital talents are paralyzed and remain unused by virtue of the unhelpful channel through which they neutralize their deepest feelings. Unlike the mourning members whose grief is temporary, these valuable members are often permanently lost to the kingdom of God because their marginal position in the church is perceived by other members as lack of interest in the affairs of the kingdom.

The Angry/Manipulative

Perhaps most destructive to a congregation is the member whose main education in the expression of angry feelings is to disguise them and use them to undermine an individual or group indirectly. There are persons in congregations who have been taught never to express anger face to face but rather to "move around" the persons from whom they feel alienated by spreading rumors and negative comments about them. I have observed individuals who whittle away at relationships by talking behind people's backs in a very hostile manner; their aim is to inflict as much pain as they have received. Since they have not been taught to confront differences with Christians in a face-to-face creative dialogue, they resort to very indirect methods of conveying their disaffection. They frequently choose the best friends of a person with whom they are at odds and proceed to raise as much doubt about that person as possible. Such a move has a double-whammy effect: It channels the strong feelings of anger toward the targeted church member and does so in such a way that even the member's friends can be confused and unsure about the person being subtly discussed.

Feelings of competitiveness in a congregation often become the source of resentment or anger that is communicated in this very indirect and unsolvable manner. Members confronted with this kind of behavior will usually act surprised that a questioner doubts their motives because they themselves have become so accustomed to this method of handling anger that they are unaware of the deep hostility behind their actions. Far more often, however, such persons have deliberately chosen this very inadequate method of expressing anger and even become very effective in their manipulative use of others to convey their strong feelings.

The major problem with this chosen shape of anger is, of course, that it is so indirect and disguised that there is no open and clear way to deal with the angry feelings. Rather than involve, at this point, only two persons in the friction, this particular shade of anger complicates a creative handling of differences by involving several persons in the issue and by using veiled communication (that is to say, sarcasm) to convey resentment.

The church of the twentieth century has fostered and encouraged this impoverished stewardship of anger in at least two definite ways: (1) We have persisted in preaching and pretending that all anger is sin and that when present it is best disguised; (2) we have most often acted out the illusion that hard feelings are best left alone, unexamined and untouched, as if that actually was a superior solution to the biblical injunction that we ought to face up to our differences with others (Matt. 18:15 ff.). What we need to risk and believe is that there are creative Christian ways to handle our deepest feelings directly without being overwhelmed or overwhelming in our message.

The Angry/Withdrawn

Some individuals have learned that the most comfortable action in the wake of anger or hostility is to "leave the scene of the accident." Accordingly, some church member's reaction to the stress of disaffection is to withdraw from the painful exposure to such feelings. At least one third of the individuals whom I have worked with, who withdrew from a local fellowship, did so under circumstances of alienation and anger. For some persons such a removal was an attempt to deal constructively with a relationship of constant friction in the body of Christ; for others the move outward was a quiet, lonely withdrawal from community and fellowship and a sense of not really counting with anyone.

Some persons who have had to fight most of their life choose, in the voluntary atmosphere of church membership, to exercise their privilege of withdrawing from conflict. One of the damages occurring in this particular reaction to anger is that no resolving of the feelings usually takes place, since in most situations there is a concerted effort either to disguise the hurt or to ignore its influence on the individual. Some fine Christians choose to live in isolation from Christian fellowship rather than explore their differences with fellow and sister believers. The unfortunate trade they agree to is a potential journey of self-pity, in the face of alienation from the Christian community, and misunderstanding on the part of other Christians who have no idea of what is behind the withdrawal. Other

Christians feel rejected or let down by those who pull away from fellowship.

Some distinction will need to be made between the individual who yearns for fellowship and understanding, yet finds confrontation more painful than withdrawal when facing anger, and the special variety of "angry person" whose pleasure and goal is to remain unrelated and uncommitted to any fellowship of believers and thus sets himself up constantly to be rejected so as to justify his irresponsible avoidance of Christian fellowship. Every congregation knows well the symptoms of the Christian circuit rider who, under the guise of "seeking a Spirit-filled fellowship," church-hops from fellowship to fellowship seeking rejection by virtue of extremely authoritarian postures no congregation would accept. Such persons are actually afraid to commit themselves in fellowship with anyone and will abort from responsible membership regardless of how much preventive Christian nurture is offered them. They are like spiritual time bombs whose rejection of a congregation is only a question of time.

Many an outreach committee has been frustrated in their attempts to reclaim some inactive church members. The committees have not understood that the nature of the withdrawal is grounded in alienation from the church. Some of our withdrawn Christians are members seething with anger who have chosen to use distance to cope with resentment. Does not their sense of isolation and loneliness need healing also?

In the next few pages we take seriously each of these manifestations of anger and try to offer with them some caring and Christian nurture that may restore broken or strained relationships in the body.

Starting Bibliography for Students of Anger

Bach, George R., and Herb Goldberg. *Creative Aggression.* New York: Doubleday & Co., 1974

Bry, Adelaide. *How to Get Angry Without Feeling Guilty.* Signet Books, 1977.

Clark, Wayne C. *The Minister Looks at Himself.* Valley Forge, Pa.: Judson Press, 1957.

Howe, Reuel L. *The Miracle of Dialogue.* New York: Seabury Press, 1963.

Jourard, Sidney. *The Transparent Self.* New York: Van Nostrand-Reinhold Books, 1964.

Lesse, Stanley (ed.). *Masked Depression.* New York: Aronson, 1974.

Neely, Kirk H. and Wayne E. Oates. *Where to Go for Help.* Philadelphia, Pa.: Westminster Press, 1972.

Rubin, Theodore I. *The Angry Book.* New York: MacMillan Co., 1969.

Schacht, Richard. *Alienation.* New York: Doubleday & Co., 1970.

Storr, Anthony. *Human Aggression.* New York: Bantam Books, 1970.

2

First Step:
A Self-Check List on Anger

Any steward or Christian mediator who is seeking a constructive ministry with the alienated must first examine his own house. A very predictable occurrence is that a minister will deal with anger in the manner with which he views this emotion in himself. Accordingly, if a pastor has been brought up to believe that all anger is sin and that there can be no good in examining such an emotion, he will obviously have no inclination to explore such feelings with his parishioners. Again, if a minister or lay person has not come to terms with his own stewardship of anger, he will find it difficult to deal with this dimension in someone else's life. One question I always ask church members from other congregations who come for counseling on anger is, "Why don't you talk with your own pastor about this matter?" Often they reply that the minister in question has either preached so strongly (note his anger from the pulpit) against anger or so condemned its expression or had such difficulty handling it when expressed that those members simply did not want to put him or themselves through the unpleasant experience of trying to deal with it.

The responsible mediator of anger will take pains, then, to discover first how he himself handles his own anger, how he feels about this emotion, and what patterns of dealing with such feelings are established in his life-style. The outline used in this book may be a good initial checklist for popular ways of handling anger (most of which, we are contending, are inadequate and destructive). Does the pastor, for example, tend to become depressed when angry and submerge his feelings into self-deprecating and destructive behavior? Is he inclined to quick temper or to "blowing up" under attack or when perceiving himself attacked? Does he tend to react more in fear when confronting anger—for this reaction will also affect his ministry with the disaffected person in his parish—or does he neutralize his feelings to the extent that he himself becomes numb to certain experiences or to even certain people (not to mention congregations)? Does the ministering lay person become easily offended in the face of resentment or anger and thus become more himself in need of care than the person to whom he is supposedly offering care? How, also, does the servant of God deal with the appearance of anger: by withdrawing, by pretending it is not there, or by facing it with candor and care and helping the experience gain responsible fruition in the lives of those affected?

Congregations and pastors could well start the process of a proper stewardship of "feelings management" by securing trained leadership for a deacon's and pastor's workshop or retreat. The wider church fellowship could also be exposed to a proper perspective on handling feelings in the body.

The pastor himself needs some ongoing consultation and/or counseling as he considers the investigation of alienation. A number of ministers are quite unskilled in their handling of their own feelings, and an opportunity

to discover "one on one" how they might effectively channel their feelings is a good, preventive, on-the-job-training
plan.

Several counseling/consultation centers are available
to the local pastor or within reasonable distance from
his parish. Individual counseling is an excellent choice;
regional and local mental health centers provide such opportunities, as well as some university communities, such
as Purdue University in our community, with a counseling
center directed by a Southern Baptist layman, Dr. Wallace
Denton.

Clinical pastoral education affords another avenue for
the pastor to explore the whole range of his personal feelings and interpersonal relationships. Such programs usually cluster around a hospital complex (as in Cincinnati,
Indianapolis, and other medical centers) or through a seminary (such as the outstanding program at the Southern
Baptist Theological Seminary and Louisville Presbyterian
Seminary in Louisville, Kentucky, under the leadership
of Dr. Edward Thornton). Clinical pastoral programs offer
both an opportunity for seminary course credit and practical in-the-trenches experience with caring for people under stress. The minister participating in such courses is
involved in weekly, interpersonal relations groups and
individual sessions with an accredited supervisor.

Group therapy is another potential training ground for
pastors. The pastor concerned with relating effectively
to his membership might recruit several other clergy in
the area and participate with them in a group counseling
experience led by a psychiatrist or other skilled group
leader. I myself was part of one such venture and found
it to be a growing and challenging pastoral experience.

Apart from such possibilities, ministers can establish ongoing consulting relationships with the mental health leadership in the community. One such group exists in our community where several clergy meet monthly at the Wabash Valley Mental Hospital and present intense case situations from their local parish under the guidance of a psychiatrist and chaplain. Such occasions have done much in my ministry to clarify confusing relationships and issues.

Certainly how a clergyman chooses to approach his self-stewardship will depend on who he is and what is most available to him in his community; the important factor is that pastors become aware of their own learned responses and emotional structure in confronting volatile circumstances in their ministry. A partial list of books which the pastor can add to his library will also give aid to his training and spiritual insight; they are mentioned at the end of chapter one.

One reason Christians have difficulty with angry feelings is that they have had little guidance in distinguishing between anger and hate or grudge-bearing. In the following pages I shall be discussing anger as an emotion springing from a *present* event, unnurtured or cultivated, and without planned destructive intentions.

Grudge-bearing or hatred, on the other hand, is anger (1) which has been consciously sustained or nurtured, (2) which has ongoing destructive intentions toward a person, and (3) which resists attempts at resolution of the feelings. While anger may spring from dated events, it only does so when an individual becomes aware of feelings suppressed or postponed for a time; hatred, by contrast, works with identified and perceived dated feelings. The person who hates has developed and cradled angry feelings to the point of giving them independent existence from any event or occasion which may have given them rise. This book cannot be concerned with hatred and its implications since by definition such cultivated feelings have no constructive purpose or intended resolution. A proper focus on anger can, however, bring us to its redeeming potential.

It is natural that the family patterns of behavior into which we are born determine to a great extent the initial responses to particular experiences. Characteristic ways of coping with and handling anger soon become repetitive patterns in our life-style. The Christian families into which many of us are born have inherited a wide technique of coping devices to deal with an emotion which Christians have far more feared and despised than understood. Accordingly, the average person growing up in a Christian home has learned more about how to hide and mask his anger than how to channel it constructively. Therefore, responsible Christian habits with regard to anger may be a difficult discipline for most Christian leaders.

Jesus Christ is, in this experience as well, the best model from which to draw examples appropriate to the expression of anger. Our Master on several occasions showed anger and blessed the emotion with potential for constructive use. Some truths we learn from his manner of handling anger are:

(1) He was concerned to express anger as a way of *concern* for someone, as when he often rebuked Pharisees and others who would use people or misinterpret truth to serve their own purposes. Over and over again Christ in the Gospels is full of "righteous indignation" and angrily rebukes those who interfere with good. One interesting

feature in his anger is that it appears most often in reaction to religious leaders of the day who were so committed to their partial truth they resisted his full truth destructively.

(2) Jesus' anger was unleashed to *correct* or *curtail* destructive behavior and not to destroy the individuals. By contrast, the anger of Pharisees and Herodians were designed to destroy Jesus as a person—a feat in which they actually half-succeeded (crucifixion).

(3) Christ *acknowledged* his anger in such a manner as to channel it toward the event or person(s) with whom it dealt, so that he never harbored it in a way that would interfere with future relationships with those with whom he was angry. He loved even those who crucified him and prayed for them as he died.

(4) The Master used his anger as an expression of *care*, as when he took his relationship with Peter seriously enough that he would not allow Peter to seduce him into following less than God's will ("Get thee behind me, Satan!").

(5) Christ did not use anger to break relationships but as an opportunity *to heal* relationships. Even from the cross, sensing the distance from his Father, he had such a close relationship with the Father that he could say, in frustration and caring anger: "My God, my God, why hast thou forsaken me?" Such a confession of the distance sin had placed between them was also a committed Son's grasping plea that such a chasm be healed by the loving arms of One to whom he trusted his dying gasp.

Such guidelines may be used effectively by today's ministering servant as he seeks to relate the good news to the alienated, hurting sheep of the flock in such a manner that he does not become, himself, an interference to re-demption and healing.

Self-examination is not an achievement to be "accom-plished" in one's ministry. It is a constant exercise in awareness so that the healing experience of the Spirit of God may flow through one's ministry unhindered by unnecessary personal liabilities. To that end the minister of God is called daily to "test the spirits" within before he "tests the spirits" without.

Equipped by the Holy Spirit, who thus enables us to discern our own emotions, we are by grace then empow-ered to exercise a healing ministry to the angry children of God in our midst. The next few chapters help us identify the various dimensions of that calling.

3

The Healing and Helping of Anger as Depression

The long-established pattern of internalizing anger needs first of all the helping hand of insight. Most Christians who become depressed when angry are not aware of what they are doing with their feelings (swallowing them). Some people do not even know that they harbor negative feelings at the time; they have turned them inwardly so often and so quickly that they do not recognize the surge of mixed emotions that may gradually or suddenly overpower them. A great deal of practice in submerging negative feelings creates a self-disturbing dejection.

The angry/depressed in the local church may be helped first by some guidance with regard to the origin of their feelings. They are usually looking *inside* themselves for their depression when a good beginning would be to look *outside* themselves to issues or people that have triggered the negative feelings.

Obviously all depression is not anger, and so the careful pastor will want to explore with the depressed the recent events that have surrounded his feelings. Preventive ministry occurs when the minister knows his congregation well enough to discern which people are prone to depression, which individuals are undergoing grief and other crises that normally produce depression, and which persons exhibit depressive behavior that is uncharacteristic and irregular. This last group of persons is the most likely candidate for depressive anger; unresolved feelings that have "weighed them down" leave them quite confused about their general disposition.

The alert deacon or church leader should also be aware of active members who suddenly or gradually change their pattern of involvement for no apparent reason. The pastor and deacon, I believe, have a calling before God to tend his sheep, and as such have the right to ask what is happening in the lives of parishioners and friends. I am frequently told by deacons and pastors that they feel uncomfortable about inquiring into people's personal lives. They believe such knowledge is no one's business, and they hesitate to investigate. The most popular comment at this point is, "If they want me to know something, they will tell me; otherwise, it is none of my business." Such an honorable attitude unfortunately ignores the fact that many people are not aware of their estranged feelings and need a friend who is willing to risk that friendship's trust by asking such a troubled person how he is doing. To leave someone to their own initiative in disclosing how they feel is the same, I believe, as allowing everyone to determine when and whether they are, in fact, physically ill. The pastor and the deacons have been entrusted with the spiritual well-being of the congregation, and a caring question by a concerned Christian brother or sister need not be construed as meddling. Would the same be said of a doctor when he asks personal questions in inquiring about his patients? Christian leaders need to assume with boldness the authority and responsibility given them by God to care for the spiritual health of the flock.

One of my favorite approaches to inquiring about the spiritual well-being of my congregation is to ask questions that allow people an opportunity for privacy. Having a choice in responding at least gives the pastor the opportunity to ask, and the answer—whatever—may be as valuable as the question itself. For example, I often ask, "Mrs. Jones, I hope you know that I do not intend to pry but need to ask you since I do not know—and am interested in your welfare: I have had the impression that you have been down lately, and I didn't know if that were just my impression of if it is so. You don't have to answer, but I am concerned. How are you doing?" Or again: "Mr. Smith, I have not seen you to talk with you in a while. I just now had a strange feeling that you were not your usual self. Is that just my impression?" Or: "George, I haven't sat down to catch up with you in a while. Tell me how you are doing and how things are going for you."

Sometimes a helpful church member will call and tip the pastor about another member who is apparently estranged or depressed. The minister can then structure communication with such a member in one of several ways: (1) he may call on the telphone (allowing some privacy) and inquire about the member; (2) he may make a point to know the member's schedule and intentionally design an opportunity for contact at lunch, at work, or at the church building; (3) a pastor who frequently visits his congregation is in an excellent position to take initiative with a home visit without signaling an alarm by his contact or presence. A call to arrange a convenient schedule for the visit is usually appropriate.

Gentleness is a fruit of the Spirit which aids the minister in exploring unnoticed negative feelings in a parishioner.

Many church members may experience embarassment at being perceived as potentially harboring ill feelings. They need reassurance and support as the pastor approaches the question in a caring atmosphere. The Holy Spirit will guide as a present help in preparing the minister to examine his own feelings in approaching any church member.

Sometimes the pastor or deacon may have secondary motives in his exploration of a given situation or his initiative toward a certain person. Common inappropriate reasons I have discovered in myself as I minister to angry persons are: (1) anger or negative feelings on my part which I want voiced or expressed by someone else in order to vindicate my cause; (2) curiosity or superficial desire on my part to observe anger expressed, primarily for entertainment's sake; and (3) a projection of my own negative feeling onto someone else because of my inability to express or verbalize the same.

The first step in the healing of depressed anger is helping the individual acknowledge and recognize the negative feelings that are present. A kind assurance of understanding will do much to aid a parishioner's self-acceptance in the face of anger. Old messages of many years are fighting the appropriate and constructive expression of these feelings. Some persons will need to be led slowly and tenderly through conversations that increasingly forgive them as they clear more and more of the confusion of feelings they contain and discover that the expression of feelings, far from becoming an unforgivable sin, rather takes the shape of forgiveness, freedom from dejection, and healing.

The pastor should also recognize that, as he introduces the question of exploring negative feelings, he is requesting permission to enter behind the veil of an individual's private life. The granting of permission by such persons for entry into this "private room" should be perceived very much as the priestly blessing of permission to enter the holy of holies in order to touch and handle the sacred elements of the inner sanctum. A church member who allows his pastor to become this kind of priest for him has offered to his minister a very significant gift of trust. Recognition and affirmation of such trust in the atmosphere of this confession should be cause for reassurance and a confirmation of the value of this healing revelation.

I use the word *confession* to describe the disclosure by a member of harbored feelings. I do not think such a word is always appropriate or helpful in early conversations with a church member who is depressed since some of their dejection is likely related to an inability to face negative feelings in themselves about others. I suggest, rather, that depressive persons be approached on the basis of their depression and that any dialogue about their feelings avoid a premature use of the word *confession*. Exploration of internalized anger may not evidence the need for confession but may upon examination reflect a very caring attitude on the church member's past.

An invitation to explore depression is probably a good first step with the dejected Christian. The depressed are often far more willing to aid in a self-examination than to enter immediately into a threatening probe of their unresolved feelings. When a parishioner has taken the initiative toward the pastor by requesting some dialogue because he is feeling low, the edge or awkwardness of starting the inquiry is removed.

The minister or deacon who has been invited to look

with the member at his depression is in a position of setting a helpful atmosphere of trust as the conversation begins. An office or area where noise is minimized is most helpful. Privacy is essential, for most depressed persons fear losing control of their feelings in public. An uncluttered mind is the most reassuring presence the pastor himself can offer, besides the obvious presence of the Spirit of God. Interruptions by telephone or otherwise will discourage a member from moving into his feelings; he has already stated his concern with great misgivings. It has taken all his courage to come to a Christian friend.

Each believer will know how best to start a conversation of this nature, but I suggest a carefully worded prayer as an introduction to the topic. The prayer eliminates unnecessary chitchat afterwards, for it sets the stage for trust and courage. A Spirit-led prayer will also be cliché-free and directed to the issue so as to introduce the topic and save the parishioner one of the most difficult steps in self-revelation—introducing the conversation. One example of how a prayer might be worded is:

Dear Lord, Mr. Blank and I come to you in the Spirit of knowing that your promise of being present where two or three are gathered in your name is for us. Grant us a spirit of openness, increased understanding, and wisdom for this time together. Give Mr. Blank your assurance of loving him throughout, and bless our conversation with purpose, healing, and deeper Christian growth. Help us to know what to talk about, and give us the courage and love that mean so much when we discuss important issues. We pray in the name of Jesus Christ, who understands all manner of feelings. Amen.

After the prayer, the minister will reduce anxiety by moving right to the issue: "Mr. Blank, I know you have a concern and that your time is important, so I thought it would be most helpful if we start off right where you are and go from there. There was something on your mind when you asked to talk with me earlier, and I want to take it seriously. Suppose we start off with what you want to say first."

Remember that angry/depressed have probably internalized their feelings because of the guilt induced by bringing them out. They need the supportive comments of grace, understanding, and acceptance if they dare explore their feelings. The pastor's attitude has a lot to do with whether a dejected Christian will let out some of the feelings that have been harbored for a long time. The wise minister will also be prepared for the possibility that the swallowed anger may be toward him and that a reaction on his part that avoids either shock or strong feelings will maximize revelation on the parishioner's side and help create a healing atmosphere of acceptance.

Depressed persons should not be forced to see their feelings or recognize them immediately. They have developed a protective mechanism for years. To uncover that defense against these fearful, powerful feelings without some support, acceptance, tenderness, and patience may precipitate a deeper experience of dejection. The pastor should allow the church member to consider his experience as possibly anger, without demanding that the listener accept such verdict. Many persons need to internalize a new idea gradually, and the careful deacon or minister will space out conversations with the depressed over five or six sessions, making sure that his last comments after each conversation offer the member hope and handles to grasp as he seeks to channel his anger. Reference to biblical people and depression (Saul, Elijah, Jonah) can reassure our people that God understands this shape of life. Our own acceptance of parallel feelings will do a great deal toward forgiving them of their mixed feelings about being angry. A word of caution: Too much reassurance and dwelling on examples of depression may have the opposite effect, leaving the member with a strange feeling that we are trying too hard to "make it all right" in his eyes.

Once the person is open to considering the role of anger in his dejection, what can be done? Careful listening is the first and most important instrument of healing the minister has available. If the member has decided to cautiously explore some feelings harbored for a while, then attentive listening will be our best gift to him. Slight interruptions to clarify, or reflective comments that reassure the church member that we are with him (such as, repeating what he has just said in summary: "so you went straight home and have not talked with her again?"), can do much to release some of the submerged feelings of the depressed.

Hearing private, precious conversation from a parishioner requires also that the pastor know that later the parishioner may have mixed emotions about his revelation to him. Afraid as they were of their own anger, church members next are embarrassed that their minister knows "this angry part of me" and often avoid the one to whom they have confessed. The understanding pastor will not press a member to a continued openness and contact since he knows that some people require some sense of privacy in order to operate adequately. A gradual reassurance that the minister does not see that member primarily in terms of his depression will take place in the casual, informal, and steady contact of general church work.

A second aid in working with the depressed is to give them options when they perceive some anger. How would they like to handle it themselves? If they are harboring feelings toward a particular individual, the pastor can suggest one of three methods for dealing with such feelings: (1) they can express these feelings to him (the pastor) in order to get it off their chest. Many persons find this approach to be sufficient as a way of releasing the demon of alienation they may feel toward someone who might not be equipped to deal with a face-to-face encounter with them; (2) they may elect, after exploring such feelings in the pastor's presence, to offer them to the person from whom they feel alienated; their advantage now is that they are more clearly aware of their feelings and have assumed some control over them, so they can offer them in a constructive manner. The pastor, at this point, can be of more help in assessing with the member what resources he has in controlling his expression of anger. The caring pastor will not release a member to communicate unbridled hostility or anger toward someone else; he will determine with the help of the parishioner *if* speaking with the third party is necessary. He will then solicit the member's aid in determining if the member feels equipped and able himself to deliver such feelings in a helpful, loving atmosphere. If member and pastor conclude that feelings are too high for delivery, the pastor can explore a third option: He may invite the member to sit with him as he invites the third party to a three-way revelation, confession, and forgiveness dialogue. He can then facilitate communication of the feelings by the members and gauge and monitor the reaction and understanding of the other person. He is also in a better position at this point to help both persons walk through the experience constructively. He can do so with a wise interpretation on a biblical understanding of anger (as not bad or good, but constructive or destructive depending on how it is used; if submerged as becoming destructive of the relationship, and if expressed and examined as having the potential for redemption and deeper love). A caring atmosphere in exploring anger between people will include at least the following:

(1) The confession by the first person of holding some anger toward the other, with a clear comment that such feelings are being expressed in order to clarify the relationship, and that the confessor is wishing: (a) to examine his own feelings toward the other person, (b) to discover whether he himself is responsible for creating such feelings, and (c) to determine if there is some issue between him and the one from whom he is alienated that needs to be examined.

(2) An expressed desire by both parties to examine the nature and the cause of the difference between them, both thus being prepared to accept some imperfect feelings of pride, jealousy, sensitivity, or resentment that calls for confessions before the other.

(3) A commitment on both parts to accept the feelings on the other's part; hear confession where applicable; offer forgiveness where wronged; and help in reconciling the relationship by assuming responsibil-

ity for misunderstandings, poor communication, or lack of concern.

(4) An established covenant to continue to be clear with each other about one's differences, to perceive the above conversation as an attempt to heal, not blame, and to dissipate suspicion and anger, not intensify its presence.

Prayer is also an essential ingredient in ending spiritual conversations of the above order. Parishioners will be relieved of their burdens by a caring, sensitive, and nonjudgmental pastor. Taking sides is unnecessary in such sessions; helping the process by clarifying what is being said and the spirit of a comment is always most helpful.

Follow-up, informal contacts with the depressed will be concrete reassurances that they are accepted and loved. If they perceive the formerly estranged relationship as having been healed in the above process, they will have learned a new approach to dealing with their anger constructively. And often since anger between persons is an expression of care, they will also be perceived by pastor and third party as risking their friendship for the sake of honesty, clear relationships, and a loving atmosphere. As pastor I would salute such courage and love with my own trust. I would let that member know how much I admire them for their attitude and maturity!

An ongoing ministry with the person who tends to swallow anger is one in which we maintain communication and help him note from time to time when he is assuming too much responsibility in a relationship and beginning to internalize feelings. When pastor or deacon notes the beginning cycle of a "downer" in this person's life, he is already ahead in his ministry with a trust relationship that allows him to ask almost immediately: "Mrs. Jones, I sense that you are getting down again; is it just my impression—or are you beginning to push some feelings down that don't need swallowing?"

Jesus Christ came to "set at liberty those who are captive," and his ministry of releasing the depressed from their unresolved anger is our continued calling.

4

The Angry—Outspoken

Perhaps one of the most difficult relationships to cope with in the Christian community is with persons who are prone to verbalize their feelings quickly and without reservation. Such individuals soon gain a reputation for being outspoken, frank, and even tactless. They are Christians who were brought up with the mixed blessing of being very direct in communicating feelings, and they usually leave little doubt as to how they feel about any given issue.

Some of these fine Christians are unaware of the intensity of their words and would be surprised that they overwhelm or offend others. At times I have taken initiative toward some church members who have "come on strong" with other members and scared or hurt them. As I relate the impression they have given others by their manner of speech, they are quite surprised that anyone perceived them as angry or forceful in their conversation. They do not see themselves as aggressive or overwhelming in relationships and are bewildered that others see them that way.

There are also some church members who have a low boiling point, become more easily annoyed than others, and express their feelings quite vocally. Sometimes such members are avoided by people in the congregation who have come to see them (note the battle-like words we often use to describe such behavior) as "trigger-happy" and are themselves "gun-shy." They speak of easily provoked members as "blowing up," "tearing into," and "attacking" others. Some people have apparently taken on what Lewis Sherrill has described as the saga approach to life. They view life as a battle to be fought and see themselves as struggling in a lifelong war "up against" the rest of the world.

Some leaders in the local church suffer from the isolation of this aggressive way of relating. They stand firmly and openly for what they believe and are so forceful in their communication that they alienate or scare others into avoiding them. They become lonely defenders of unpopular causes—causes which might have taken on more attraction were they not advocated in the particular manner with which these people speak and act. Many of our finest Christians become isolated, bitter "minority spokesmen" in our congregations, who see themselves as rejected by most (if not all) people, and alone in the battle for a given truth.

The way we are brought up to relate in a home has some effect on how we come across with others. I remember as a boy, growing up in Brazil (where my parents were missionaries), that I would sometimes walk into a friend's house and feel that I had just stepped into a private family feud—only to discover that their family simply spoke "with vigor" whenever they wanted to make a point and meant nothing destructive about their loud conversation. Some people have been brought up having to assert themselves in order to be heard and speak out more from a need to be taken seriously than to control or overwhelm.

Unfortunately, many good people are unprepared for their bold way of stating their views.

There is at least another set of people whose outspoken feelings declare a deep disaffection from the folks around them. Some individuals have felt deceived or rejected by people over and over, until they come to expect distance from others and actually wish such distance out of self-protection. Such protection takes on the form of loud, brittle comments or of verbiage that is designed to attack another in order to cause him to pull back or withdraw under fire. Such church members are the angry lot among us who have ceased to care how they come across to other Christians and wind up actually testing the friendship of others by assessing their ability to survive their verbal barrage.

Are these simply so-called Christians who have actually never offered their attitudes and behavior to God? No doubt all of us are in constant need of the Spirit's presence within us to transform our conversation into kindness, gentleness, and peace (Gal. 5:21 ff.). But one often overlooked factor is that Paul himself, in describing the fruit of the Spirit, refers to goodness as a virtue which balances kindness. If the latter refers to a gentle spirit, the former is used in describing Jesus' caring firmness as he drove out the money changers at the Temple. The truth here noted is that Christians have often confused goodness with a certain backboneless sweetness that betrays the sense in which Paul (and Christ) celebrate the disciple's unwillingness to compromise truth for the sake of comfort or harmony. In other words, some very direct Christians (the Nathaniels in our midst) are at times exercising a fruit of the Spirit ignored by more tender, but often more compromising brothers, who shirk their call to stand firm on a given truth and substitute for it a sweet but dishonest comment. Some church members we know have become quite adept at approving questionable behavior or attitudes by agreeing verbally with members rather than stating their differences and standing up for a truth even in the midst of the potential conflict aroused.

Perhaps a proper recognition of the Nathaniels and the Thomases in our fellowship is in order. When Nathaniel was told by friends that they had found him "of whom Moses in the law, and also the prophets wrote" (John 1:45 RSV), he responded by saying: "Can anything good come out of Nazareth?" (v. 46). Christ's comment upon meeting him next is not a word of offense at Nathaniel's bluntness but a commendation of his honesty, "Behold, an Israelite indeed, in whom there is no guile!" (v. 47). His affirmation is for a person who speaks his mind, so that in him there is no deceit. Such persons, although at times offensive to our more tender *sin*sibilities, are people whom we can count on, for we know exactly how they see a certain issue and will not "pull punches" in order to protect us from needed truth. Christ was very comfortable with those who spoke with no intention of deceiving—unlike the Pharisees, who constantly had secondary motives in their communication with him.

What I am suggesting first of all is that some outspoken people in our congregations are the salt of the earth, for they bring into a fellowship the crispness of spontaneous responses which hold undiluted, honest opinion. They are unwilling to say what everyone else says simply to be in agreement with the majority; they are always their own persons, and their opinion should be cultivated by pastor and church leadership alike—for more than likely, right or wrong, it is an opinion which, if subjective, is at least a different point of view than the all too often yes member's unweighed comment.

One first constructive step in a ministry with the outspoken members of our congregations is that of interpretation and understanding. If we, first of all, are able to distinguish for ourselves between the destructive, ill-advised comment and the honest, if brittle, well-intended word, then we as pastors and leaders in the church can begin to exercise the wise discernment of not responding to the outspoken in a way that will reject them or misunderstand them.

A proper discipline for any minister or deacon is the ministry of careful listening so that as servants of God we "pick up" on the kernel of the truth as it is spoken by God's flock. If we are able to note the guarded isolation from which some of our members speak, we may be able to respond to them in such a way that we include them in our circle of trust—rather than push them away (as their manner of communicating might entice us to do). By responding not so much to *how* things are said by the outspoken Christian member, but to *what* the intention and the underlying motive is in the words, we can begin to draw out the best in even very alienated persons.

One such instance occurred not too long ago when a pastor was meeting with the finance committee of his local congregation. One very forceful member of the group started to make his point; his manner of speech was so abrupt that members of the committee began to react to him in a characteristic way. They began to shut him out, to argue against him, and to reject what he was saying.

The man in question was already accustomed to feeling rejected by members of the congregation and actually offered his advice in such a "take it or leave it" fashion that he set himself up to be resisted and denied. What he didn't realize—and what the other members of the committee did not realize—was that he was being resisted not so much for *what* he was saying but for his *manner* of saying it. His proposal was, in fact, outstanding and practical, but his valuable insight was about to be lost because of his approach.

The minister in question quietly broke into the argument, requesting a word for clarification. He had listened carefully to the man's thought and sensed some merit in it. He said, "Brother Jones, let me be sure I understand what you are suggesting so we can all be sure of what we are discussing. If I understand you right, you are suggesting that . . . ." In a clear and concise way the pastor repeated Mr. Jones' suggestion but reworded it to remove both tone of voice and possible sharpness. He was repeating the comment for three reasons: (1) he wanted his outspoken member to know that he had paid attention to him, knew what he was saying, and found value in it; (2) he wanted the committee to hear the man's opinion for its best intention and evaluate it without bias or reacting to the personality of the man (as much as possible); and (3) he wanted to listen to the idea himself, once more, to be a responsible evaluator of its merits.

When the pastor briefly restated Mr. Jones' suggestion, he made sure that Mr. Jones had a chance to indicate that what was said was, in fact, what he himself had meant in the comment. When Jones confirmed the summary by the pastor, the interruption had broken the verbal argument game that had erupted, and the members began to say that they had misunderstood. One member of the committee, another outspoken person himself, suddenly commented that the idea now made a lot of sense. Soon all members were evaluating the idea brought forth by the man and were enthusiastically confirming it.

What happened in this meeting? First, a very isolated man presented a good idea that was almost lost by his way of stating it. What could have been a confirmation that he was, in fact, not appreciated by the group, turned out to be a session in which he was affirmed as offering the best suggestion of the evening. He left sensing that he was appreciated—probably for the first time in a while. Some members of that congregation in that committee also left with a new dimension of Mr. Jones they had missed. How did it all take place? Quite simply because one servant of God listened carefully and exercised a ministry of interpretation for his alienated brother.

Some members in our congregations need a regular ministry of interpretation and understanding, for they leave behind them a path of wounded Christian citizens along their way. They are unhappy, lonely members of the church, who want fellowship (and need it desperately) but work overtime against it.

A caring deacon or minister can do a lot to help the outspoken appreciate better how their way of dealing with others affects other people. It is not unusual to find a church member who is not aware that he overwhelms or affects people in such strong ways. A caring friend can take such a person aside and communicate to him how his behavior of word—though not meaning to offend—makes it difficult to get the hearing he wants. A private conversation for such purposes is clearly superior to embarrassing anyone in public. One-to-one conversations frequently reduce threat and suspicion enough that the minister's intention and care is clearly felt. Again, very little is more important to such an outspoken person than to perceive that the servant of God with him cares for him and wants his good.

A good, general rule is to be gentle but direct in such conversations. Little is gained by beating around the bush; the average outspoken person is likely to be most accustomed to directness himself. I find it helpful to say, "John, I noticed something as you and Jim were talking that might explain what I sensed as some trouble in your understanding each other. If you have a few moments, I'd like to go into the office and talk with you about it." Most persons of this nature welcome such opportunities.

Once in the office (door closed), I usually get right to the issue: "John, a few minutes ago while you were talking with Jim, I sensed some discomfort on his part—I don't know if you did. Because I know him fairly well, I thought I might comment on what might be happening that made it difficult for the two of you to understand each other. Jim is a quiet and controlled person, and I believe he has trouble hearing you because you tend to be rather direct and straightforward when you speak. I'm not sure if you know it, John, but it's a quality in you I appreciate— you are very honest and straight with what you say (affirmation)—unfortunately, some people are just not prepared to deal with that forthrightness. It comes across to them in such a forceful or overpowering way that they miss the significance of what you are saying just because of the way you said it. Now I'm not sure if you see it that way, but I guess I wanted you to know what I thought was going on from where I sat. If that is what's happening, it's a shame for Jim not to be able to hear you for fear of your way of being direct—and it's also a shame if he winds up pulling away from you when he's the kind of friend I would commend to you. What do you think of what I'm saying?"

The good news for the outspoken and direct church member is that we will neither reject him outright nor take him lightly. The anger of many a church member had often been grounded on a steady foundation of neglect and inattention. If as servants to God we can translate their alienation as a declaration of isolation and sense of "being out of fellowship" with the rest, we will have taken important strides toward creating more harmony and mutuality of respect in the fellowship. Most outspoken people have a larger bark than bite and are quietly yearning for a Christlike spirit who can take a son of thunder and transform him into a loving disciple. Such people are, in fact, if appropriately cared for and befriended, among the most loyal and dependable church members in your fellowship and mine.

Having spoken about anger in verbal people as a declaration of disaffection, I feel the need to point out that there are a good number of persons in our congregations who are very alienated Christians. They feel isolated from fellowship and ignored; they feel angry and rejected. They have usually decided to reject back, and the resulting war between them and certain members who will always do battle with them over the same issues (ignoring the underlying confession of alienation in the anger) is rarely productive.

When church members sense themselves repeatedly battling over different issues with the same set of persons, one first redemptive question to be asked is whether the issues have really been dealt with—or bypassed over some precipitating problem. I mention such possibility because I regularly see church members fighting over an issue that, if they could be honest with themselves, is far less important to them than their underlying feeling of resentment or alienation over some previously unresolved and unexamined issue. One telltale evidence of such residual anger is when members resolve their issue dispute and continue to show signs of anger. I am impressed with the regularity of mutual rejection in congregations, as when members disputing over an issue continue to attack one another long after the issue is history.

Such stored up feelings need also the attention of a caring servant of God, and an alert deacon body and minister will pay careful attention to how their sheep relate to one another. Since 1 John reminds us that it is impossible to love God and hate our neighbor, the issue of anger with God needs to to discussed. One comment about warring brothers and sisters is first in order.

When Christians persist in their alienation and verbal hostility toward one another (or toward the pastor), the most healing action that a shepherd can take is to take the initiative toward that person and raise a question. I know no other helpful way to deal with alienation and anger than to inquire about it. Never assume that you are right about its being there, but ask the person about whom you are concerned. For example, "Mr. Martin, I asked to chat with you a few moments because I was feeling somewhat uncomfortable about our last conversation. It seemed to me that as we talked there was some sense of anger or resentment in the way you talked to me. I am not saying I know it's there, but I'm asking you if you felt it? If so, is it something we need to talk about? I may have offended you and not known it or caused you rightly to be angry and be myself unaware. What do you think?"

Give a Christian brother or sister opportunity to back away from such an encounter. Although the outspoken person will tend to welcome the chance to verbalize his feelings, you may be dealing with someone who is easily threatened by the thought of anger or someone who needs time to sift out just how he is feeling. Some fine Christians are so conscientious that they will not acknowledge such feelings at the moment in order to gain some control over them. Their intent is good, for they want to avoid saying something they will later be sorry for or so getting out of control that they themselves are in a rage. The chance and invitation being given, the member who wants to talk but had not identified his feelings now may do so (with permission to feel that way from you).

A comment with regard to differing personalities is in order. Sometimes the people of God have confused "loving" (as Jesus Christ commanded all of us to do toward one another) and "liking." The Master's injunction with regard to love is defined as a commitment to wish for and work for the very best for my brother. The comment about love says little about my personal feelings of attraction for such brother. The Samaritan loved the attacked traveler on the road to Jericho, but there was no indication (or requirement) that the victim like him or become a close friend to him. God brings us together in the crossroads of life "to love one another on" in the Spirit with which Jesus Christ did. Unfortunately we try to demand of unnatural relationships in the church that they be more than that—that we in fact be *equally attracted* to various members of the body of Christ.

What I am suggesting is that some members of your congregation will be more attracted (by personality and manner) to some members than to others. We will feel more comfortable around some people than we will around others. In no way does such a happening mean that we are not exercising Christian love, for primarily love means caring enough about my brother to will and work for his good—as I do for my own good (love you neighbor as yourself). Accordingly, let us allow for differences in our fellowship that help us to strive toward loving all, but not requiring of all that they like all! Paul himself exhibited this distinction I am trying to explain when he chose not to take his second missionary journey in the company of John Mark and Barnabas, preferring Silas (Acts 15:36 ff.). I believe Paul loved John Mark, and in his caring for him he was realistic enough to know that he could not get along with John Mark in the rigorous intimacy of a missionary journey to Gentiles. So we in the church can be called to love all of the fellowship but not demand that personality differences be ignored in the process.

Such a world suggests that we allow some distance between ourselves and some brethren with whom we do not see eye-to-eye. While never ignoring them or slighting them, while always striving to hear their contribution and to take seriously their gifts, it is not good wisdom or love to require of us or them that we force a pretense of likeness with them in order to carry on the bond of fellowship. God is gracious enough to a congregation that he gives each a variety of disciples, all of whom by his purpose are able to relate to some people in the congregation in a creative manner. The wise shepherd helps his sheep find fellowship with one another in their common bonds; one helpful ongoing ministry of the deacon body is the continuous introduction of member-to-member—helping the fellowship to knit bonds of affinity and affection.

What about the church member who fits nowhere? is a serious question for the caring pastor. There are some members (outspoken) who, by virtue of their attitude and outlook, make it very difficult on themselves to belong. A cautious word here for the earnest servant of God: There are some people who choose not to belong or participate in fellowship and work constantly for distance and rejection. Their goal is to be rejected, and they will undermine all attempts to reconcile or include them in fellowship.

Jesus Christ spoke of these who would reject the message of reconciliation which disciples would deliver. He instructed his disciples to spread the good news in each city, and, if rejected, to shake the dust off their sandals and move on (Matt. 10:14). Such an injunction applies, I believe, here too. We must never hasten to dismiss the opportunity for reconciliation and fellowship; we should try our (loving) best to always keep doors of fellowship and bonding open. One important dimension of such work of reconciliation is to make note that reconciling has been attempted and has been rejected by one of the parties. To shake the dust off one's sandals was a clear, concrete evidence of rejection of hospitality; the host was made responsible (by this gesture) for the interrupted fellowship.

A pastor or deacon involved in the work of harmonizing relationships should pause at the point where an individual refuses such, and take note that it has been attempted and that if in the future such persons change their mind, the door for reconciliation and belonging is always open. A servant's attitude at this point is significant. If I do not wish to hear your anger or deal with your sense of rejection, I may even communicate relief that you have resisted fellowship or conversation. It is important that I, as a minister of Jesus Christ, be aware of my own attitudes and motives in this step.

Once disaffected members have been approached for an opportunity to relate to pastor or fellowship and have refused, I would place the responsibility for initiative on that person next. We do not need to insist on fellowship, or we invade private territory. A brief comment of care from time to time (perhaps a note to the person) is sufficient indication that he, not we, has no desire for communication.

One final interpretation about outspoken members needs to be said. There are some people whose manner of speech is purposefully designed to create some distance for them in personal relationships, and they use their way of talking and directness to create some privacy from undesired intimacy. Accordingly, the Spirit of God will need to guide us with discernment and understanding in such particular needs. We should not move in too hastily on the established private terriory of these persons in trying to bring them closer to us—or someone else—when, in fact, they are wishing more distance. Not everyone needs the same closeness or the same number of intimate friends. We need to affirm and respect the member whose meditative experience with life requires less personal contact and closeness with people.

Rather than make a membership feel guilty about its inability to reach certain members, the pastor or church leader can interpret the appropriate contentment which some members find in special friends. He can also explain to eager associates that they are not personally being rejected when such persons resist their overtures for fellowship. The minister can even make cause to celebrate God's gift in the lives of certain people in the Bible who were very selective about contact with others (Elijah, Daniel, John the Baptist, and so on). In so doing, he blesses the meditative personality in the church, still an oddity today in churches that equate activity and social communion with Christian commitment.

God's calling to minister with and to minister to the outspoken in our churches is a unique challenge. The pastor who has had to mediate between two such persons in a congregation knows the trying, but important, role he can play in channeling the gifts of the guileless into constructive vessels for use in the kingdom.

5

The Angry—Afraid

There are two primary manifestations of fear that are caused by anger. The first is the church member's fear of his own feelings of anger and a resulting dread that such feelings would ever be released and take control of him. The other is the fear of that same emotion loose in others—out of control. Either experience creates what Soren Kierkegaard called the anxiety within a person which we often call *dread.* Let's examine both experiences and talk about a redemptive ministry to each of them.

The person who fears his own feelings of anger more than likely has been offered some very poor models as expressors of anger. One of the enduring messages of early childhood is passed on by parents who are so afraid of their own feelings of anger that they stifle or attempt to erase its evidence. If the Christian home could learn to distinguish between destructive display of anger and appropriate expression, much of this unnecessary dread and inappropriate teaching would disappear.

Christians need to realize, for example, that God actually made all emotions and that he created anger for several good reasons. We have already mentioned earlier that anger can be an expression of care. A comment now needs to be made about anger as a constructive venting of frustration and as a channel through which a child learns his limitations. When a small child, for example, encounters a will other than his own and is faced with being forced to do something he does not want, he adjusts his behavior by facing his limitations. In the adjustment, he is disappointed, frustrated, and angry that he cannot have his way. The question of whether he is frustrated and angry is irrelevant. Everyone who is controlled or stifled from doing what he wants at first experiences both emotions. The question, then, is not whether a child will get angry, but how he shows that anger. The angry frustration can be an avenue of adjustment and acceptance of the reality that he cannot always do as he pleases; or the anger can be submerged and intensify (harbored) so that every once in a while, when overloaded with it, the child will have an outburst of uncontrolled anger and probably be destructive to himself, to others, or to something.

The process of personal rebellion against God has this element of anger in it. We all face, at one time or another, the fact that we cannot do as we please; the inevitable limitation creates a sense of frustration and resentment. The adjustment to accepting our limitations (and God's protective love in those limitations) is made easier by the acknowledgment of our anger and frustration—not by our pretense that we are pleased with our limitations. Eventually we realize that our parents (and God) limit us in order to protect and help us. This realization makes us both very grateful and relieved that we were restrained. But in the process of learning about our feelings when restrained, we may also be impressed that resentment or anger is wrong. Such learning comes from parents who cannot accept anger as normal during frustration and, rather than allow its expression as a healing step toward acceptance of self-limitation, come down hard on any expression of anger. The result is that we are often taught quite early that there is no room at all for anger in our lives and that it is dangerous enough an emotion that it should be done away with if present. Since it won't be done away with without some channel, it is stored away and becomes an arsenal of explosives that could go off at any moment if left unchecked. The angry afraid people usually walk around with a good store of anger that they are tremendously afraid of and that they fear may "go loose" and render them out of control. Of course, by walking around without giving anger any proper channel, these fine, scared people are intensifying the problem. What they fear the most (unchecked feelings) is what they are most setting themselves up for.

How can the angry/afraid be released from this dilemma? Only with a caring, trusting, and deliberate ministry of confidence and understanding. The pastor needs to set some realistic goals in a healing ministry with the fearful. We should not expect such church members to quickly reverse a process of fear they have harbored for so long. The servant of God may do well to set as his first goal a reduction of the fear in this member's life. To help him function with a reduced sense of impending dread about himself around others is an effective purpose on its own.

Some people will gain confidence enough to even acknowledge and express some of their hidden anger. They will likely only do so in an atmosphere of firm support and unwavering nurture. Like the depressed person who has internalized anger so that it would not be loosed on others, the angry/afraid is desperately anxious not to unleash a feeling he fears very much.

One reassuring first redemptive effort by a ministering person is to be someone who is so in charge of his feelings that he becomes a model of reassurance to the church member fearing his feelings. By a good model I do not mean an individual who has so controlled his feelings that they do not show, but a person who can be a proper example of anger that is expressed but neither overwhelming nor destructive.

A good pastoral model can show his feelings without losing control of himself. He can indicate when he is frustrated without overwhelming someone. He can be aware enough of the other's capacity to handle such feelings that he does not offer too much. His caring invitation to witness or receive another's feeling is a source of comfort; whether the church member chooses immediately to examine his own feelings depends on the degree of fear present.

Persons who fear their own anger struggle with a lack of forgiveness about their feelings. They will need to be reassured that such feelings will not be held against them and that they will not be punished for expressing them. They live either in regular dread that such feelings will overpower them or have so disguised them that they themselves do not understand their effect. Some of the fears often associated with the need to control anger are the fear of a rage, the fear of losing one's mind, the fear of hurting someone, and the fear of death. Let's examine each of these common anxieties in the pastoral setting.

Some persons who have stored away their anger for a long time come to boiling points when they explode and then tend to throw what they call a temper tantrum or say things that later embarrass them. Such unpredictable occasions only confirm their fear of anger and their deeper commitment never to allow such feelings expression again.

What such people ignore, however, is that a rage is most often the result of feelings that have not been allowed normal expression and that finally break out with unusual force like a dam bursting out destructively because the proper pressure values did not release enough water to avoid the overload.

The healing experience for those who fear a rage, then, is to learn from a trusted Christian that their option is not to sit on their feelings in such a way as to totally stifle their manifestation. The creative control of frustration, anger, and resentment comes to the point of being able to release and express it in small but manageable doses. The person who fears temper outbursts can first be led to understand how their tight control over any expression of anger is the main cause of the explosive way in which it finally erupts.

When a person begins to understand that he can avoid such rages by dealing more directly with resentment and anger, he will need some guidance as to when and with whom he can express it. Obviously not an emotion to be expressed just anywhere, anger is best housed in the company of a trusted community that can both handle and channel it as the strong emotion that it is. I often wish the church were the people and the place where such potentially harmful feelings could be brought—and diffused like a bomb. Unfortunately, most churches I know are neither prepared for nor accepting of such a mature calling.

If the community of believers would exercise more "perceived forgiveness" with regard to its members, the fear and embarrassment of getting out of control would be dramatically reduced. What church members often fear most is the judgment or criticism of other church members. The possibility of acting in such a way as to become an embarrassment has such a powerful effect on people, in general, that they will go to extremes to avoid such pain. Unfortunately, the storing up of angry feelings so that they will not be seen constitutes a sure way for them to exercise more and more pressure on the person until the fear of an explosive reaction, or the reaction itself becomes paralyzing.

The occurrence of such outbursts can be minimized with a church member who trusts a deacon or a pastor enough to share his frustrations and resentments with him from time to time. The solemn sanctuary of a trusted conversation between two people of God can become the regular place for a proper stewardship of anger that no longer takes control of an individual. Feelings can be periodically drained before they grow to such a proportion that they scare a person into a fear of blowing up.

The ministry of listening openly to a friend who is very afraid of his feelings can also be the healing process whereby this same friend gradually gains confidence in his own ability to accept such feelings in himself. The fact that a man of God (or his representative) will listen and take seriously such feelings has a way of saying that such feelings are worthy of being heard—that they will not overwhelm the listener. If the fearful saint sees his friend walk with him through some of these feelings that have been pent up so long, he will begin to reassess their label of unacceptable. Thus forgiveness and understanding enter the picture, and healing begins to take place.

The gratitude and relief with which a person often receives such freedom from this fear is often amazing. Ministers and other servants of God who engage in this "ministry of diffusion" know the meaning of Christ's words to his disciples at the well where he had been talking with the Samaritan woman: "I have meat to eat that ye know not of" (John 4:32). Christian friends who share the plight of their brothers gain deep joy in witnessing the release of the captives in his name.

A second common fear under the pressure of angry feelings is that of losing one's mind. Church members come to me every once in a while with a keen sense of apprehension about strange internal confusion. They are afraid that they are losing control over their faculties, and the fear is a haunting concern that frequently is related to how they handle frustration and anger. Some people work so hard at controlling undesirable feelings that the pressure from doing so causes all manner of strange feelings—especially the rapid change from one set of emotions to another, the loss of memory (as when the thoughts are so strong that a person pushes them aside), and the dwelling on a feeling or an event until it drives one crazy.

Again, the healing and understanding ministry of a level-headed Christian friend is the best antidote to such fears. A servant of God who understands the nature of such fears is a helpful reassurance to a Christian friend plagued by such dread. To find someone who is not himself fearful of a friend in these straits gives confidence and strength to an embattled spirit.

A person frightened by the possibility of losing control

of his mind needs, beyond reassurance, some tangible ways to work more effectively with his anger. Where an opportunity for looking at the pattern of fear with regard to such feelings is possible, some insight can be gained as to how such panic occurs. Again, the key to a proper release from the grip of anxious fears is the church member's openness to accept and acknowledge some of his anger, frustration, and resentment.

I find very often that a teamwork approach to the dissolving of such fears is helpful. By teamwork I mean the partnership involved in the healing team of physician, psychiatrist (or appropriate therapist), and minister. A medical doctor is a handy consultant to whom a church member should be directed for regular physical care. When major and long-term fears are associated with the angry feelings we have been talking about, a reliable counselor in the community can do much to explore these feelings in the context of a safe distance from the church—where the church member may feel both conspicuous and embarrassed.

The pastor has a double calling in such a healing partnership. He is called first to be a "minister of introduction" as Wayne E. Oates has so aptly put it. Many parishioners are at first wary of a counselor or psychiatrist, and the known and trusted minister can be the bridge to a new relationship with an unknown counselor. To call and refer the member to such a professional and to alert him to the particular needs of the person can do much to reduce the anxiety of working through such "starts." In addition, the pastor may offer to call the counselor while the church member is with him and thus have the member know how he is being introduced and that the counselor is aware of the need.

The second calling of pastor and servant of God in such situations is to continue his supportive ministry with the church member. A regular contact (phone call, quick chat at the door, infrequent and short appointments) will assure the church member that the pastor is neither "ditching" him nor is so rejecting of his feelings as to no longer wish to see him. Care must be taken to make clear to church member and counselor that the pastor is going to act as a supportive shepherd—not an additional counselor—in the healing ministry.

Some church members carry the burden of fear that their uncontrolled anger might lead them to hurt someone else. The possibility of injuring a loved one is often on their minds, and devout church people have been known to shrink under the constant dread of such verbal or physical violence. There are, as just stated, two ways in which they may fear their feelings taking charge in a destructive manner: by injuring someone emotionally (words) or by injuring someone physically.

I talked not too long ago with a member who felt that he needed to go around daily asking people for their forgiveness over some comment made. He was so tight and controlled that he was putting out a lot of energy keeping his feelings in. When the feelings overwhelmed him, he blurted out a comment that he soon regretted. He was both tired and embarrassed with his confessional routine and entered conversations with fear and trembling that he would let go and do verbal damage.

This friend needed some help in dealing with stored

up resentment that apparently was quickly camouflaged by a long history of rejection. Whenever anger or frustration arose, a quick maneuver inside of him shifted the feelings into the back room but allowed them to accumulate until the whole back room broke out into the living area.

Helping this man accept some of his negative feelings, appropriate angry reactions, and natural frustrations is part of the shepherd's calling. Often the most helpful experience for such church members is the presence and initiative of a Christian who gives them permission to verbalize some feelings about which they have long felt guilty. The fact that a great deal of guilt accompanies some of this pushed back feeling is the cause of more fear. The person's reasoning is something like this: If I really look at all these feelings that you say I am afraid of, then they will come out, and I am afraid that I will not be forgiven for them.

Although the fear of others' rejection is not to be ignored, often church members struggle more with their own inability to forgive themselves (rather than God forgiving them or others understanding them). A wise deacon or pastor will remember that guilt and shame accompany such experiences of divulging feelings. A minister or servant of God who is not prepared to offer forgiveness at the point of such fearful confessions is not ready to sit in the mediating chair of God's mercy seat. Self-examination is here again in order.

People who fear hurting others physically may or may not have good cause for their fright. The incidence of spouse beating and child beating is not confined to persons with evil motives. The church of Jesus Christ has a good number of members who suffer from uncontrolled passion that leads them, under stress or deep frustration, to strike out at loved ones. They are themselves their greatest judges; they do not need our further condemnation. What they do need from us is the pledge of our continued love for them in their struggle, our supportive ministry in their guilt, and our guidance by the Spirit of God in helping them find more responsible ways of dealing with anger and frustration.

The church member who consistently loses control and hits a loved one needs careful ministry. The shame and fear already mentioned in such instances is aggravated by the negative connotations we give to such behavior. Such a member already fears rejection from within and without, since he already condemns himself and anticipates immediate ostracism if found out. The caring minister should avoid any use of labels or descriptions that reflect judgment and emotional condemnation if he is interested in being redemptive with such persons. Accordingly, such popular labels as "child beater" and "wife beater" have no useful purpose in a minister's conversation with or about another Christian.

The pastor can incarnate the good news if he takes initiative with such fearful people in a caring, Spirit-filled atmosphere. To approach a Christian brother or sister as a friend and to say that you are concerned with him about his struggle for self-control and that with the Spirit of God you want to offer your support, prayers, and assistance in whatever ways might be helpful is a good start.

Christian friends in this kind of predicament need a good portion of assurance in the midst of their self-condemnation. While never condoning such behavior, the minister of God is steady in conveying God's comfort in their anxiety, his forgiveness in their guilt, and his strength in their weakness. The primary factor to note in physical abuse is the extreme frustration which this person is feeling. People who strike people physically are confessing that they have exhausted all their reasonable ways of dealing with their anger and have nothing left with which to counter but physical force. They feel helpless; after they hit someone, they feel even more helpless—not strong or proud.

What can we do for them? Having given them initial understanding, we need to take their struggle seriously, for it is a major problem. We need to help them understand that their feelings are, in fact, controlling their behavior in a destructive way, and—that it is possible to reverse or discontinue that pattern. Many such persons talk to me with the same kind of defeated spirit with which an alcoholic describes his plight—they feel helpless and powerless to change. Like the alcoholic (or any other person who has surrendered control of his life), they need first of all to realize that they need help. Individual therapy is indicated in most cases, and the pastor's most significant contribution may be at the point of getting the parishioner to see this need.

A second step in the controlling and healing of physical force in anger is for the person to assume responsibility for his behavior. I often hear the common myth from people that "they cannot help it, it's just the way they are." Many a heritage has been blamed for behavior which has been learned through years of poor child training. Unless a chemical or physical factor is involved, people who behave and act a certain way do so by having learned it from their first models—usually their parents. Almost all temper tantrums and uncontrolled behavior I have seen can be traced back to parents and *how* they taught their children to deal with anger.

Such a comment is not intended to criticize parents or to lay blame on particular groups. Rather, it is intended as good news again. For if I say that such forceful behavior is learned, then it should be evident that it is possible to *un*learn it! And when I suggest that it should be worked on seriously (with counseling), it is because, unchecked, it becomes the source of learning for the generation currently growing up in that person's household. If left unattended, the same teaching pattern (a poor model for handling anger) will simply be passed on to the next generation. Is that not what the Bible means by "visiting the iniquities of the fathers upon the children unto the third and fourth generations" (Ex. 20:5)? Little mystery that we teach our loved ones poor habits—and then pass it off as "poor blood." We should, rather, take responsibility for having learned and take steps to unlearn it, if not for us, for our children's sakes.

The shepherding deacon or pastor remains faithful to his relationship with such members as they consult with a counselor. He can offer the continuity of a family of God who cares throughout the difficult and painful process of relearning. He can offer reassurance under discouragement, support under frustration, and another firm relationship with which the struggling Christian can practice appropriate expression of feelings.

Church members are not just afraid of hurting other people. Sometimes their hidden anger can be so disguised that it takes on the fear of death. I have had the awesome privilege of sitting with good Christian friends who were plagued with the fear of death, and no Christian reassurance of their forgiveness in Christ seemed to relieve this fear. Tender and careful pastoral conversations led to a discovery that sometimes Christians have so pushed back their angry feelings that they have taken on the strong proportions of a "death wish."

Christians who struggle with the fear of death may or may not be dealing with suppressed resentment, but many persons who wrestle with such fears are actually contending with unresolved anger. The shape of such fears may take the direction of fear of dying themselves or may take on the fantasy of anticipating the death of a loved one or friend.

The struggle with one's own death is an attempt to control the destructive urges inside. Good people who cannot admit anger toward others may develop intense fears of dying, sometimes in an effort to kill that undesired feeling in themselves. Reassurances of God's love often are unhelpful to such persons primarily because they evade the central issue: How can God forgive me for hating someone (or him) so that I really am not sorry that I hate? Or, God cannot possibly forgive me because I cannot forgive myself.

The caring deacon or shepherd who is in charge of caring for such pained individuals would do well to suggest the possibility of anger in that Christian's life. Again, giving a person the opportunity to reject such an idea allows him room to resist—then accept the truth—no sooner than he apprehends the forgiveness of God through the caring relationship. This point cannot be overemphasized: the minister whose nonverbal cues (frown, intense pressure, accusatory posture) communicate judgment or rejection of these feelings will not evoke them from a member. Only love "calls out" uncoerced confession and begins the crucial Christian process of reconciliation and redemption.

Other times unadmissable anger toward loved ones may take the form of the fear of their death. I occasionally talk with parishioners who are haunted by the dreadful possibility that a particular family member may die. Their fears about such possibility are beyond the normal separation anxiety which any good Christian has about someone he loves. What is happening in many such cases is that deep resentment toward that person has gone underground, and the not permissible feeling is appearing disguised as a fear of such person's death. Again, unknowingly, this church member is quietly confessing that he has enough anger toward a loved one that in a sense (though never in reality, unless pathological) he wishes the person dead. For the loved one to die would solve two issues: In the haunted Christian's mind, he would be relieved both of the person who is the object of his resentment and of the guilt of having any more anger— since they would be dead.

Such fears of death require competent professional help. The responsible pastor may have the spiritual and counseling tools for such care, but most often he may neither have the skill required nor the time for such counseling care. A reliable Christian psychiatrist or counselor in the community can render invaluable assistance in such a case. The pastor, again, remains on board as the tandem caring person. The continuity of his contact and ministry with this person assures him that he is loved—throughout his greatest fears—into Christian freedom.

One particular experience I had at a Youth retreat may

serve as an example. A few years ago a teenager in the congregation where I served slowed down as he walked by me to a game, and said: "Were you ever afraid that your dad would die?" I registered the question, recovering from the surprise of the revelation and the setting (although young people are very much like everyone else in this regard: They often say very important things quite casually to see if anyone notices). I replied that I had, since as a kid I remembered fearing that my parents (missionaries) might be killed in an airplane crash. He stopped long enough to record my answer and went on to play ball. Later on at lunch, I made a point to sit near enough to him to keep in touch. In a lull in the conversation, as we were finishing the meal, he added (as if never having interrupted the conversation): "I think about it all the time." The public setting made the nature of the conversation awkward, and I waited for a chance when he was alone to say: "Does that kind of thought about your dad's dying happen a lot, Sandy?"

He shrugged it off and said it happened quite often but that he didn't let it get to him. He obviously (moving away) wanted to be left at that point, so I backed away, storing the self-evaluation for future notice. Many people test us with small doses of truth to see how we handle them.

About three weeks later he "happened" by my office, having asked me once or twice when I was around. He sat down, stood up, told me how he rarely saw his father, how much the man traveled (in government work), and how they used to play together a lot. He then commented that he sometimes dreamed that his father was killed and that he refused to go to the funeral. He apparently dwelled on such fears often. As I stood up to walk toward him, he said he had to go—then mentioned that he had been looking at my library once or twice (books on psychology of religion) and that there was a book I needed if I was going to understand him at all. Then he left.

On my desk three days later was a book entitled *Why I Hate My Parents*. I read it, pausing only in wonder that he had told me so much in such a small gesture. I saw him a few days later in school (where I drop in to keep in touch with the kids), and he asked me if I had gotten the book. I invited him to drop in and tell me more and that began a process of about seven drop-in visits. He was surprised that he had stored up such resentment toward people he loved and then was surprised that I would hear it. I once asked him for permission to share his deepest need with his parents: their understanding and attention. He wondered that I would want to do so, allowed me to, and a few days after I had done so tapered off the visits. I saw him two or three more times after, and at the last contact he said that the fears about his father's death had somehow almost disappeared. Contact with the parents revealed that they were spending more time with him and that he was growing in maturity.

Sandy is one of many fine people whose anger and resentment take on the dimension of a death wish and then the fear that they are powerful enough that their halfwish might come true—that they might lose their loved one. Behind such fear and anger is a stronger feeling, love. Such members of the body need to know the redemption that sets them free from the burden of such misunderstood feelings. And is not the body of Christ the proper instrument of such healing?

If anger disguises as fear getting out of control, of losing one's mind, hurting someone, or wishing someone dead, then such experiences also produce fear in other people. The angry/afraid in our churches are not just fearful of anger in themselves; very often they are just as threatened by such feelings in others.

Consequently, some people in our congregations dread others because they are living reminders of their own suppressed anger. It is natural to fear emotions in others which we ourselves have trouble handling. So it will happen that some members in our churches will simply not want to be exposed to some members in the church mainly because these members scare them by not being in control of their strong emotions. The pastor and the shepherding leadership of the church can exercise a ministry of protection in the flock, for some members we know are fragile enough that they should not be required to field other members' feelings.

Minister and concerned Christian friends can often act as a buffer between members whose manner of relating may cause anxiety and fear to others. The wise and caring pastor knows his sheep and can sometimes oversee a proper stewardship of contact between persons.

Sometimes a church member may show unusual anxiety or fear around certain people, and a sensitive person of God can help him work through these fears by a proper understanding of his own struggle with feelings. A responsible shepherd will also be alert, in such situations, that he is not shielding an immature young Christian from the needed growing pains of learning how to relate with Christian brothers and sisters of different points of view. It would be sad for pastor, church member, and body if the man of God constantly protected certain members from a needed confrontation with ideas and persons who might challenge unfinished Christian convictions into a deeper understanding of God's way and will.

Perhaps the most obvious summary of these pages is again contained in the wisdom of Scriptures. John reminds us that our struggle with fear has to do with our imperfect understanding of the nature and application of Christian love (1 John 4:18,19). Anger and resentment need never overwhelm us if they are contained and channeled by the "greatest of these," love. And in the living out of love as the atmosphere in which fear and anger are examined, "perfect love casts out fear. For fear has to do with punishment, and he who fears is not perfected in love."

6

The Angry—Numb

Unlike those who have feared their feelings, another group of Christians has chosen to freeze their feelings and thus anesthetize themselves from their effects. The detrimental result, however, is that in doing so such persons neutralize gifts and talents that go unused and unemployed.

There are many Christians with frozen assets in our congregations, and a number of these fine people are unaware that their resentment or anger is the major cause for their aloof and unproductive behavior. When I discover a church member who is currently inactive in my congregation, one of the very first things that I do is to ascertain that person's service record in the congregation and in his own Christian pilgrimage.

Whenever I find a strong history of religious commitment, involvement, and service that either suddenly or gradually stopped, I begin to search for causes in this change of activity. What I often find is an experience of pain and anger that has taken the shape of an anesthetic distance from involvement. What these people are saying with their actions (though often quite unaware of such emotions) is that the alienation or anger they feel is so painful that they choose to draw back from fellowship and involvement and protect themselves by a curtain of distance that innoculates them from the hurt they have suffered.

Behind such pain and "apathy" is a deep sense of alienation from people they have loved dearly over the years and who have meant a great deal to them. But the resentment and shock over some event has led them to pull away emotionally from the body, and while remaining physically present, they exist in a neutral state of inertia and uninvolvement with regard to the work and movement of the church.

Some Christians operate with a high degree of control over their emotions and have established internal procedures to prevent venting anger. They take seriously the biblical injunction that "a soft answer turns away wrath" (Prov. 15:1, RSV). However, in following such a precept, they often deal only with the immediate expression of anger and ignore the damaging aftereffects that arrested resentment produces.

Perhaps a comment on arrested feelings will alert us to this particular occurrence. By *arrested feelings* we mean the experience where individuals are unable to move beyond certain emotions. They sense a feeling or reaction, and wishing not to deal with it, curb its expression or manifestation. They usually then choose to ignore such a feeling (most often anger) and assume that by pretending its disappearance they can command its demise. Unfortunately, as we have stated several times earlier, unattended feelings simply do not just go away, they usually take another form or shape of expression—just like water may become vapor or become ice.

The subtle effect of arrested feelings is that they are not often recognized for what they are and become barriers to effective Christian relationships. The first source of the difficulty is that the feelings are left unexamined, and the person harboring them never really graduates from them. Unable to move on, such a person is trapped by unresolved attitudes that are constant burdens.

The Christian factor in such arrested emotions is that of forgiveness. Individuals who have difficulty forgiving others often dwell on past experiences so that they never leave them. They continue to relate to certain people out-of-dated emotions and events and never quite move beyond them. Unable to walk through the anger in such a way as to let go of it, such persons waste precious energy and commitment on unnecessary silent battles. They cannot forgive, literally, because they have not forgotten.

A second loss in such situations is the stewardship of these persons' gifts and talents. Arrested feelings incapacitate good Christian people. My personal experience with most of these fine members is that they have a strong history of involvement in church leadership. When an issue or problem interrupts such activity, both church and individual suffer.

Mark was such a person. He had spent years of service in the church and was considered by many to be a very happy Christian and family man. He often participated in the fellowship activities of the congregation and even planned some of the funniest of his class's Sunday School parties. He was popular among the members and rarely had a sad word to say about anything.

But one church council meeting in which he was absent the pastor "came down" rather heavily on people who were not holding to their commitments by not following through or by being absent. Mark heard the pastor's comment through a friend, and together they interpreted the remark to be for Mark. The next time the minister and this committed member exchanged greetings, there was an unpleasant coolness and distance in the relationship.

Mark missed the next three meetings of the council, though he faithfully attended all church services. The pastor, having inquired with others about his absence, eventually called Mark, said he had been missing him at council meetings and asked if he could get together with him over a cup of coffee to "catch up" on their relationship. Mark agreed; they met the next day, and the pastor brought up the subject of Mark's absence and what it might mean.

At first Mark was hesitant; he suggested that a very busy schedule, work pressure, and family needs had kept him away. Toward the end of the conversation, as the pastor rose to leave, Mark almost inaudibly commented that he disagreed with the way the meetings were run and didn't feel that he was the right person for the role he had. When asked for a suggestion about the running of the meetings, he responded by saying there probably was no good way to do it and that what he might dislike the next member might appreciate. Frustrated, the pastor left Mark and returned to his office with a sense of having failed to discover precisely what the problem was in this member's relationship to his church position.

The chairman of the nominating committee informed the pastor three weeks later that he had Mark's resignation in hand. Mark gradually pulled out of voluntary involvement in several projects and soon was attending the morning worship service only, quite irregularly. His quiet manner in the church projected an image of unhappiness and frustration, but repeated efforts by pastor and deacons brought no new insight into the marked change in his behavior. Two years later he continued his physical presence in the congregation, but his spirit was absent.

What had happened to Mark? His mysterious behavior seems a puzzle to many, yet his experience is repeated dozens of times throughout the year in many congregations. Mark was a sensitive man, and he was apparently offended by the remarks which he perceived were said by his pastor about him. He chose not to face his feelings of resentment (or perhaps even justified anger, if the remarks did refer to him, with his record of service). Instead, he withdrew emotionally in his pain and chose to express his anger by sabotaging an important relationship to a committee and a relationship with his pastor.

Persons like Mark, if asked by a total stranger to describe their feelings under such circumstances, would have difficulty getting in touch with their anger. As a friend of mine once put it, such people are often so out of touch with their own resentment that they themselves are bewildered by their numbness. Nevertheless, the unexamined feelings stand between them and the person or the event they resent—like a "blob of eight hundred pounds of Jello" that no one can get a handle on and move out of the way.

Such people usually miss supportive ministry for themselves because of their unexplained behavior. Concern or interest in such members soon turns to impatience and frustration. The result is that once again persons most needing ministry and support tend to create an environment in which they are the least likely to receive it. And when the pastor is the object of this resistance, their pain is compounded, in that he is usually the person called by God to be most sensitive to such feelings of alienation, but being the target of alienation, he is not likely either to understand or to respond caringly.

Two particular variations in the manifestation of anger as numbness also need to be described. In our churches these two expressions of anger create much frustration for those called by God to minister and encourage. Let's examine these two experiences before we make comments about the healing of numbness as anger.

John Boyle and others have identified the "tar baby" type of behavior which certain members use as a regular way of relating in the church. Some folks have gotten so accustomed to "playing dead" in our congregations that they have developed the ability to use the experience as a lethal weapon. Innoculated as such persons are from behavior or feelings that would hurt them, next they develop the ability to use their quiet resentment in such a way as to frustrate anyone who would minister to them.

Some of the most caring members I know become extremely frustrated at trying to develop a ministry of concern with the angry/numb who simply will not respond to any expressions of care. Only the most patient and loving people survive the withering experience of extending friendship and concern to people who never respond. The tar-baby reaction to ministry is, simply, the old story from James Chandler Harris' *Tales of Uncle Remus* of Brer Rabbit and Tar Baby, the dummy made of pitch. Brer Rabbit was a sociable fellow who was out to make friends. He simply couldn't stand someone who wouldn't respond to his overtures. He encountered Tar Baby one day on his road. Tar Baby was just standing there in the middle of the path. Extending his hand, he introduces himself—but gets no response. Again he says hello, only to be met with silence. Irritated with this rejection of his friendship, he decides to threaten Tar Baby and tells him that unless the dummy speaks to him he will strike him. When no answer comes, he aims a blow with his right hand that smacks Tar Baby right on the face, and his fist promptly sticks to the dummy. "Unless you let go of my hand I'll hit you again," Brer Rabbit cries. No response meets with another blow from Brer Rabbit's other hand—and a second "stick." Brer Rabbit is now so angry that he kicks Tar Baby, only to find himself with one, then two feet stuck. He finally decides to butt him with his head, and at that is totally paralyzed by the unresponsive doll.

The caring member who seeks to minister to the angry/numb takes the risk of "getting stuck" every time he tries. People who have a need for people have to be careful that their willingness to minister does not so control them that they *must* minister to everyone. Pastors are particularly vulnerable to this kind of dejection and irritation when they have tried their best and feel totally frustrated with the angry/numb. Since (according to several recent polls) ministers have a high need "to be loved," we run the risk of feeling rejected by such persons.

Such behavior by parishioners needs to be met, then, with a good balance between Christian concern and cautious aloofness. The pastor needs to continually communicate his care and interest in such members but never allow himself to depend on their response as a measure of his ministry. The angry/numb can be one of the most frustrating individuals to work with, and a safe rule of thumb for the caring Christian is that he should remain distant enough that he is not "sucked in" by the inertia of these anesthetized people.

I often encounter this challenge in Christian ministry with the potentially suicidal people. Angry as they are with themselves, sometimes these hurting people move into a state of neutral in order to cope with their inner pain. They incapacitate themselves and then hope someone else will make all the decisions for them. One popular mistake at such a point is to step in and make decisions for such paralyzed parishioners; they gladly accept our parental care and also allow us the full responsibility for any consequences.

The angry/numb are often oblivious to the anger controlling their behavior. They think that they are physically not well and would much rather attribute to other causes the explanation for their apathy. They will usually deny any anger, and their most frequently chosen words for feelings is *hurt, disappointed,* and *indifferent.*

One other manifestation of numbing anger needs to be mentioned. A popular title among psychologists for indirect human resentment is *passive aggressive behavior.* What they mean by such a term is that some people use their anger in such a hidden and passive way that it is disguised and subtle. Some of our angry/numb church members use this kind of behavior in the church, often bewildering the most adept Christian leadership.

Specifically, angry persons who choose to neutralize their resentment can very quietly express their anger by sabotaging relationships, committee work, and leadership functions. From time to time I am impressed with the effect that one person can have on a whole project by simply playing dead with his responsibility until the matter is beyond repair. Some of the most popular passive aggressive action takes place with church members who, not feeling consulted on a particular issue, will allow it to move on until a certain decisive moment or decision is being made and then quietly refuse to give the necessary work or support for it to move on.

Political people are accustomed to the way in which some elected officials will simply allow something they do not like to be so delayed in action that it is "killed" by inattention. Such a passive way of dealing with differences or issues is destructive mainly because it never focuses on the anger behind such actions—or lack of actions.

Thus some very angry church members will frequently accept a position (or a plan they do not like in their family life) and "sit on it." Other members then become angered that they have not pursued it—when they never agreed to it at all. They express their personal power by freezing their part in a relationship, or a project, so that it cannot move forward and dies.

What ministry is most effective with the angry/numb? Obviously a most important first step would be to help the neutralized and numb church member to consider the possibility that resentment or unresolved anger may be at the root of his incapacity to function as usual. Unfortunately, some people never accept the possibility that anything different or arresting is going on in their lives and refuse further assistance from the pastor.

The church member who rejects intervention in his numbness needs some long-distance pastoral care at least. Trusted friends and deacons can be alerted to his condition, so that this person is given the proper love and support he usually works against receiving. Expecting to be isolated, the angry/numb are often surprised by the grace of a caring friend who loves them as they are and refuses to equate their worth with their paralysis.

The church of Jesus Christ is a hospital for such anesthetized people. Any given congregation can function adequately with as many as two or three such persons per hundred functioning members. A nominating committee chairman can be another caring ally in a ministry with the angry/numb; such persons should never be placed in positions of church leadership and probably should not function in a committee with another person like themselves. A healthy, committed group of workers can lovingly carry such a person on a committee, but a leadership position would both bring the inevitable anger of the congregation upon such a person for not functioning and make the person himself even more angry—perhaps paralyzed—for failing in leadership.

Such quiet ministries must often take place without the church member's cooperation. Too many of God's children are so unaware of their resentment that they are unable even to aid in their own healing. Loving by Christ's standards assumes the call to "go the second mile" and help those who paralyze themselves. Our challenge in such situations is to care for people who cannot respond and thus deal lovingly with those who probably may not love back.

A second step in ministering to the angry/numb is to make some distinction between the numbness of bereavement and that of unresolved anger. Those who are moving through the numbing effects of grief and loss tend to experience temporary innoculation from feelings. Time is a factor in making this distinction, for grieving persons move on to other stages in the process of a personal loss.

Another fairly common characteristic of grief numbness is that the griever is aware of his loss of feelings and even wonders whether he will ever return to a normal condition of sensitization. The angry/numb, on the other hand, is usually unaware of his condition of emotional anesthesia. When he is aware of his emotional detachment, he usually cannot link it to a particular event as the mourner will since he has just experienced a loss which has precipitated his grief.

Trust is an important ingredient in the healing of arrested numbness. The church member who experiences such detachment is very often a private person with regard to his emotions, and any divulging of feelings will depend largely on a relationship of trust he may have with pastor or deacon. Accordingly, one early strategy of ministry by pastor may be to determine who in this church member's circle of Christian friends is most trusted by the numbed brother or sister. A caring minister might then approach this friend and involve him in the primary communication with the detached member.

Several times I have been in the position of an outsider who was completely dependent on such a faithful member to minister for me to such hurting, isolated members. I have often relied on the caring, trusted friendship of a member whose love for a removed brother has caused him to be the mediator of God's grace and companionship to the isolated. A close friend can do what a pastor or deacon may be unable to do and that is to develop the possibility that the numbed may venture to confide in them about some of their pain.

When the member who has removed himself emotionally from the fellowship is willing to evaluate his feelings and his insulation, a healing atmosphere is in the making. The caring minister needs to establish at such point a sense of openness and absence of condemnation in hearing out the offended member's story. Again, pastor or church representative need not defend the church or another member's position in the description of the event precipitating the distancing. Whatever explanations or clarifications are needed about any given misunderstanding will have their appropriate moment. What is needed first is a clear demonstration by pastor or other ministering person that he understands the hurt (and angered) member's position and feeling at the time.

The process of healing actually begins when an isolated member discusses his bottled up feelings that have led to his paralyzing behavior. Even though he may be unaware of their effect, the stifled feelings, once expressed, will relieve him of the burden of carrying them unattended.

Pastors in a position of hearing a long-time sealed expression of feeling need to be prepared for it to be out of perspective. A temptation parallel to trying to argue or defend a certain position expressed is that of reacting too fast to the quantity of stored-up feelings. If we react too hastily to information revealed with some misgiving, we will only reinforce the numb member's suspicion that he should have kept the lid on those feelings as he first intended.

When the hurt revealed by a member has occurred between him and another member, the pastor may next seek his permission to act as a mediator between them. The caring person should never force this meeting of minds but should indicate to the angered member that he sees some benefit in clearing some of his feelings in an atmosphere of constructive mutual listening. He can suggest that he will be willing to invite the offending party to a conversation with the angry member, and that he himself, the pastor, would be glad to sit in and facilitate the constructive and healing function of the conversation.

If the member is not prepared for such a direct, open dialogue, the wise pastor would do well to back away and give the member some room. A steady ministry of support and encouragement may bring the member to a place where he feels comfortable enough to suggest a conversation with the pastor present.

Preliminary ministry with the angry/numb most often involves a regular contact which offers the increased opportunity for venting of feelings. We need to recognize the fact that ministry to the anesthetized member is a long-term, slow process. Dick is one good example of such gradual healing.

Dick is a long-term member of the congregation that had, over a period of time, become quite concerned with the direction the church was taking. At a particular business meeting an action being considered by the church was being discussed, and Dick felt strongly about it but never commented at the meeting. When the vote was taken, the church adopted a course of action contrary to his point of view, and Dick left the meeting very distraught.

During the next few weeks he and his family seemed to drop out of most church functions but worship, and

Dick's responsibility as chairman of a committee seemed to get less and less attention. A friend of Dick's called the pastor to ask if he knew that Dick was very frustrated with the church; the pastor was unaware of Dick's feelings and suggested that the friend inquire further to determine if a visit by the pastor was appropriate.

Further interest by the friend led pastor and concerned friend to conclude that Dick wanted no contact by the pastor and really preferred not to discuss the matter further with his friend. Pastor and good friend agreed to continue to minister to Dick from a distance and give the matter some time.

After several months the minister asked Dick to join him for lunch, gave him an opportunity to discuss family and church in general, and to offer the pastor any suggestions as a long-time member of the congregation. Dick offered no suggestions and merely commented that he wasn't as close to the church as in earlier years (important comment!).

Several months later Dick continued an obvious pattern of distant participation in the church. In the course of two and a half years the friend visited with Dick, brought out slight feelings of discomfort and disappointment in Dick, and gently backed away every time Dick hinted at feeling pressed.

The pastor continued brief, informal encounters with Dick, structuring opportunities for him to comment on his impressions and feelings. From time to time Dick would indicate a source of concern, then move away swiftly from it in conversation. Three and a half years after his inital detachment, Dick is gradually assuming some leadership function again in the congregation. He has never discussed his differences of opinion with me and has never talked about his frustration and anger with anyone (to my knowledge) save his quick comments to the Christian brother who has so ably ministered to him.

Some church members never move beyond this experience of numbness and live out a pattern of insulation that remains a way of life. Patient, loving ministry with such arrested behavior is all the minister can expect to offer. When persons limit our ministry by their resistance or inability to deal with such feelings, they effectively keep us from channeling the whole grace of God in their lives.

The constant temptation for a pastor weary of apparently unfruitful ministry with such persons is to wash his hands of such relationships and conclude his contact with them. A caring supportive ministry by the church body needs to be a constant source of support for pastors and other ministers of the body at this juncture—since their encouragement and sustenance will do much to feed the pastor in such withering ministries.

One further comment needs to be made about the experience of spiritual anesthesia. Several church members over a period of time develop what, for lack of a better name, I call a spiritual innoculation that affects their entire religious outlook. They are usually angry with God, but since they have great difficulty expressing such feelings toward him, they choose the silent spiritual withdrawal as an expression of their resentment.

Ministers who care for the spiritually numb help most when they do not feel compelled to defend God. A quick reading of the Word of God will reacquaint us with the fact that many a devout believer questioned God in the

Bible and that many a psalmist expressed his anger at God. God is big enough to handle such feelings, and he does not need our defense of him. Angry, frustrated people sometimes need to be able to express their frustrations at God (who already knows how they feel anyway) in order to deal in a redemptive way with arrested and destructive feelings.

The spiritually numb need to recognize that God can handle their anger and that they can be forgiven for it (most who disguise their anger by innoculation are confessing that they believe that to be angry with God is unforgiveable). The skilled representative of God can help those trapped by their own feelings to deal with their differences with God, without having to sever their relationship to him. One great fear in the expression of anger is that a relationship will be broken. To help a parishioner through such fear can release him from resentment he will otherwise harbor for a long time.

The spiritually numb very often are struggling with an event or experience which they blame God for, and they are not sure they can forgive him for it. The caring minister, who has established the truth that God can handle any of the emotions he invented, can next help the person sense what particular issue he is struggling with. I have often found that one of the major causes of resentment toward God stems from an incomplete theology that makes him responsible for every act that takes place on the earth.

Church members need, at such point, the caring instruction of a pastor/friend. Those who have been taught or believe that God is responsible for everything need to mature their theology to include an understanding of man's freedom under God, an awareness of the demonic at work in our world, and of accident or chaos.

Some people forget that God limited himself by giving man freedom when he created the world and thus is not responsible for a lot that goes on in man's name. When someone goes out and gets drunk, then drives recklessly and kills someone, it is blasphemy to say that God killed that victim. A human being who took it upon himself to exercise his freedom in a reckless manner killed that person. God would have wished it otherwise, but he has controlled himself from interfering in this life with man's freedom—even to do himself in.

When disease and illness claim a life, they are only confessing that God has allowed the demonic and destructive to have freedom in this world. To say that God caused such diseases is to claim or assume a great deal about him. The early biblical writers did believe that he caused everything—and they were aptly refuted by Job (his entire book is to counter the assumption that all tragedy is from God, and from misdoing); Jeremiah (who clarified that the consequences of sin are destructive, but that God was not their originator, man was); and Jesus (who spoke clearly about how the loving Father's sun and rain fell equally on the good and evil).

Finally, a careful reading of the Scriptures would remind us that God stepped into chaos (Gen. 1) to make it purposive and orderly—that he has been doing so ever since. We lack an understanding of a theology of *accident* in our faith: Some things are caused by God, some things are caused by us (good and evil), some things are demonic (evil), and some things are chaotic or accidental (the world is neutral, out of order). God steps into each of these events to make good out of evil, but he does not cause evil to occur.

I hope this brief summary of an oft-forgotten biblical truth may be of value to the pastor seeking to free some member from the unneeded anger of attributing all causes to God. The concerned pastor will listen, interpret, and offer God's counsel in these matters assisted by the Holy Spirit of God.

Some numbed church members are angry with God because they believe he has abandoned them. A caring ministry of steady contact and care will help act out God's continued love for these people. Trust and openness will allow the pastor, in this instance, to also interpret that God's silence does not mean his absence, that his waiting often is his wisdom, and that his answers often do not come in the shape we pray for. His presence is the constant promise he has offered us—not freedom from pain or hardship. Jesus Christ is again the perfect model of life, who never allowed himself to avoid the events of life, but walked right through them, even to death—and resurrection.

Patience and loving continuity are the Christian factors which often nurse the worst of spiritual distances back to life (and resurrection). Deacon and pastor can exercise their best ministry of reconciliation and mediation at precisely these most painful of junctures in people's lives. There are few experiences more rewarding than the opportunity of seeing God's arrested children come back to life under love and care through the Spirit of God!

Finally, there is a group of persons in our congregations whose shape of angry/numbness renders them virtually ineffective in that particular congregation. Some members simply find it too hard to forget or too difficult to return to the former church involvement they had prior to their angry withdrawal. When such a possibility is apparent to the pastor or deacon, it is wise to help that person connect with another fellowship in which he may find new communion.

It is at this point that many fine Christians are lost to the fellowship. Unable to serve and fellowship in their former churches, they find themselves in suspended animation, belonging to no communion. They are lonely and isolated, and they need encouragement and support in seeking a new fellowship.

The pastoral call in such situations is to exercise that ministry of introduction that can help a wounded member transfer his service to another congregation. The pastor should be very careful that such an option is initiated clearly out of a sense between member and pastor that future service in their present church is damaged beyond comfort or practice. The minister needs to be careful that he himself is not seeking to get rid of an undesirable member and that he is not heard by that member as trying to wish him somewhere else.

When it is very clear that a given parishioner is never going to find fellowship and service again in his old church because of an experience of pain or anger, the pastor can suggest to him that he consider active involvement in another fellowship. The minister who has kept alive a ministry of information and community awareness will be aware of several possibilities for fellowship for this isolated sheep, and he can then offer helpful suggestions to the member about which churches to consider. He can also call the pastor of such congregation (as I usually do), introduce him to the member, and update the pastor on the experience that has led to this move. Stating the issue before neighboring pastor *and* detached church member will reduce the suspicion that the pastor is trying to get rid of the parishioner and afford an opportunity to reaffirm the member by speaking of his qualities before the pastor in consideration (and not going into unnecessary details about the situation or people involved).

Some people who are angry/numb will refuse to leave their connection with their present church, yet function minimally in it. The love and care of God need to continue for them, even if they barely respond. In the long run, some church members never respond to pastoral care or encouragement and choose to live lonely, hurt, isolated lives. In keeping with the freedom God gave all of us, we, like him, accept what we will not force to change and grieve what could be—if only the pained, numbed children of God would accept imperfect relationships, forgive, and live beside us in grace.

7

The Angry—Manipulative

One of the greatest challenges in Christian service is a ministry to alienated persons who express their anger through manipulation. The struggle in ministering to these church members is that so often their feelings are expressed indirectly, and pastor and caring friends must often deal with deception and hidden resentments.

A ministry with the angry/manipulative starts with an understanding of how they express their anger and what it means. Students of human behavior will tell us that some people have learned quite early in life to hide their true feelings because of the pain or punishment inflicted on them when they are open. They are often left with few alternative ways of coping with their anger, and they soon resort to indirect ways of letting it out. Indirect communication accomplishes two purposes in such a case: (1) it allows expression (though camouflaged) of deep feelings a person has, yet (2) it permits the angered person to frequently remain anonymous and hence go unhurt after having expressed his emotions.

In some ways the church member we discussed in the last chapter as a passive aggressive individual is manipulative in his use of feelings. He uses his power in a given circumstance to thwart the work of the church or the desire of an individual. He does so because he is angry with that person or mad about an event or because he wants to change a course of action without taking an active part in doing so.

Jane, for example, has been deeply concerned about the direction a Youth Church Training group has taken. Her daughter is in the session, and the mother resents the discussion topics and the attitude of the leaders. Her concern is genuine, but rather than speak to the Youth leaders about her feelings, she methodically chats with each of the parents of the youth involved in the group, suggesting in her conversation that she really questions the wisdom and the experience of the leaders. She continues to give the leaders no indication of her discomfort but next talks with the pastor about the leaders and questions their judgment and ability.

The pastor asks the parent if she has raised these questions with the leaders themselves and is told that she did not want to offend them and had not spoken to them. He asks if she has discussed the matter with anyone else and is told that she perhaps mentioned it to one or two parents (he has already received two phone calls on the issue). He promptly suggests a meeting of the parents involved, asks Jane to be present, and calls the leaders to indicate the development and the need for some dialogue with the parents. The leaders agree, the meeting is called, and the pastor attends.

In his opening comments, the pastor suggests that all present are committed to the Christian growth of the youth and that a dialogue was called to facilitate understanding and make their common goal more effective. He avoids any implication of an inquisition but sets the stage for responsible confrontation and clarification. He asks Jane to verbalize her concern, and she immediately indicates that she herself has no concern but that she had heard a concern from other parents. Since at least one parent of each youth is present, the pastor asks for any of them to express this concern. There is silence for several minutes and then one of the parents volunteers that he knew little of what was going on in the Youth group, but that he had become concerned after what he heard from Jane about what was being discussed.

After several comments that seemed to share a common source of concern, the parents entered an open discussion of the questions they had heard about the couple and their approach. Jane even entered the conversation, and her resentment was at times apparent. The pastor recognized her frustration, the meeting moved on to discuss ways in which the parents might support and enhance the Church Training efforts and the leadership involved, and a positive atmosphere began to prevail. The leaders' first suggestion in regard to support was that the parents always communicate directly with them when they felt a concern about the program or the approach.

What the pastor did in the above situation was to control a potentially damaging event in the life of a congregation. Able if inexperienced teachers may often make mistakes in their church work; most likely they will learn from each experience if given the proper atmosphere and support. But these same people may be crushed and forced away from our fellowships if not handled with love.

For my doctoral dissertation I visited with eighty families which at one time or other became alienated from a local congregation. One of the most frequent criticisms they voiced about their congregations concerned an unloving and critical attitude among the members. Many of these persons had experienced destructive and distancing behavior from people who were supposedly on the same team and working toward the same cause.

Jane's manner of operating is not uncommon. She has perhaps a genuine concern for the youth in her church, but she may be far more desirous of forcing the leaders out than of helping them to learn in their experience. What the pastor did in his intervention was to turn the indirect communication toward open conversation. He also called in all the people already affected, in an effort to curtail rumors and control the issue. His desire was to involve all concerned people in a healing venture in order to resist destructive and premature judgments.

Unfortunately, pastor and caring ministers often are not told of such developing problems in a church until far more damage and pain has already taken place. As pastor I am on the constant alert for people who are working around people in their efforts to undermine an issue or an individual. Jane's pastor forced her to face her own feelings and these leaders in an atmosphere of potential good. He also channeled her resentment into a setting where it could be expressed openly and honestly. She, like many manipulative persons, may refuse the opportunity to use such open avenues of communication; but she can, henceforth, not use people or the same issue again against an individual without facing her own feelings in the matter. She may possibly have also learned a more constructive way of handling her dislike about a given issue or a person.

The aim of a ministry with the angry/manipulative is not first to change their pattern of expressing anger (they have learned such habits over a long period of time and will need a long time to undo them). It is first, rather, a ministry of "destruction control" so that the manipulative gestures of the member do the least amount of damage and are curtailed early in their divisive effects. The pastor usually needs to identify the source of rumors and "movements" that are designed to counter individuals or issues indirectly. He may do so by asking any member who brings him information or concerns to examine the relationship or the issue with him.

One effective healing gesture is to ask two parties in a controversy to sit down and talk with each other face to face. The pastor who offers his presence in mediation of such encounters can do a great deal in reducing the anxiety of such events. He will also minimize distorted information by holding both parties to assumptions and statements they have been making in the other's absence.

When an angry/manipulative member is forced to own his feelings in a relationship, he will usually cease indirect approaches to handling his anger—or he will know that pastor and member involved know him as the source of such feelings. In my experience with the alienated who use manipulative devices to channel their feelings, I have found that confrontation and clear expression of feelings on my part is most helpful.

Church members also need protection from being used by these individuals. A concerned group of Christians, who is on the alert against gossip and generalized rumors, can do much to curtail manipulative use by angry people. Unfortunately, there are enough church members who can be seduced into conveying ill-founded rumors and thus cooperate with the manipulative church member.

Suspicious or easily threatened pastors and other leaders can be easy prey to the manipulation of some angry members. The member who is adept at manipulation will often approach the minister with an issue which he claims affects the pastor, his well-being, or his relationship to the congregation. Such deceivers usually "suck in" the pastor with tales of alarm and fear concerning his parish, and the unsure pastor may find himself running around putting out nonexistent fires in deep consternation—much to the secret amusement of the manipulative member, who thus indirectly expresses his anger at the pastor.

The naive or gullible church leader is another vulnerable partner to manipulation. Church members will often come to pastor and church leaders with some of the most destructive information or rumors available and have minister and church in a stir over distorted and unexamined comments. The biblical injunction from the Master is an appropriate advice in such ministry: "Be ye therefore wise as serpents, and harmless as doves" (Matt. 10:16).

The most effective spiritual antidote to a rumor is to contain it at its inception. The alert minister of God can control destructive or irresponsible comments in his parish by suggesting to any bearer of information about another that he sit down with the pastor and the persons mentioned and clarify what is being said. Such a clear opportunity to investigate an unsure word about someone has a way of "smoking out" the intentions of the bearer.

There are some people in our congregations who adopt the responsibility of carrying news about others to the pastor on a regular basis. A good relationship with the people in his church will help a pastor at this point, as illustrated by an incident that occurred to a minister friend of mine.

Not long after he arrived at a particular church to serve as pastor, my friend was made aware that a certain member seemed to corner him and introduce information about other people in the church. Most of the time the second-hand news was distorted and damaging, and the person offering the information usually shrouded her commentary with secretiveness and suspicion.

After a few months of this kind of behavior, the pastor was met one day after church by this person. She brought up some feelings she had heard another member mention about the pastor, suggesting in the process that several other members also felt the same way. Looking over his shoulder, this minister happened to notice the person mentioned in the conversation and called her by name across the room. To the shock and dismay of the first parishioner, he held her gently by the arm for a moment while he said to the approaching member, "Mrs. Marsh, you and I usually are very open with one another, and I always appreciate that spirit. Tell me, did you have some particular feelings about our telephone conversation the other night?"

The second member openly and freely declared without threat that she had no hidden feelings and expressed an opinion about the conversation which counteracted the rumor just received. Now, with the two women present, the pastor turned again to the bearer of bad news to ask if there had been some misunderstanding, stating to Mrs. Marsh that Mrs. Ash had thought she was of a different opinion.

With the two ladies present, soon the rumor was dispelled, and the pastor took the moment to indicate to both that he certainly appreciated their being open with him, that he had every desire to hear from either of them about *their own* feelings, and that he was going to rely on both to interpret themselves to him. He never heard any more news from Mrs. Ash after that, save for a polite commentary on herself from time to time (usually in response to his inquiry and to assure her that he was not angry with her and cared for her).

This woman had learned rather abruptly that her pastor was not going to put up with distorted and manipulative conversation. Not everyone would wish to approach this matter in such an assertive fashion, but I am going to suggest that too much tenderness and protection will hurt and feed an angry/manipulative person.

Persons like Mrs. Ash need to be controlled in some direct and firm fashion for their own sakes. They have learned somewhere along the way that the best way to handle their hostility is to "move around people," as psychologist Karen Horney said. The fact, however, is that such a maneuver is a very poor way of dealing with one's feelings for several reasons.

In the first place, people who use other people to vent their feelings are clearly misusing the privilege of a friendship by riding another identity with their own opinions. They should not impute on others feelings that are their own; everyone has the right to his own feelings and should not have to deliver anyone else's emotions for him.

In the second place, manipulating someone else to deliver one's feelings is an irresponsible way of handling feelings. Mature Christian living demands that a person own his own emotions, thoughts, perceptions, actions, and expectations. To slough them off on someone else is to disown them and thus to deny a portion of himself. Angry feelings need both acknowledgment and confession, and projected feelings cannot be properly acknowledged or expressed.

In the third place, a manipulative way of using people to express one's anger is a sure way of never resolving deep issues and pains in a constructive manner. Manipulation has the temporary reward of doing someone in and obtaining revenge. The problem with revenge is that it is short-lived, and the individual seeking it will soon need to develop another project or attack because his feelings have not been sufficiently dealt with.

In the fourth place, the manipulative use of people to begin or continue a rumor (or a truth, for that matter) has the damaging effect of multiplying the experience of pain. The more people are involved in the discussion of a person's life, the more pain and damage is done. Jesus Christ himself applied the principle of the fewest possible involved in personal matters (Matt. 18:15). The first directive when a difference occurs between people is that the matter should be brought up strictly between those involved. Jesus then went on to suggest the involvement of a third party if necessary, and the whole church community only as a last resort.

Sensitive listening is an excellent guard against premature evaluations. One of the most popular traps we fall prey to is the erroneous assumption that because someone said something it is so. Apart from trustworthiness or integrity, the wise minister of God will always ask as he hears the information, Who is the source, and under what circumstances did they hear this? and next, What is their goal in telling me this?

The fact of the matter is that many manipulative persons are not fully aware of their behavior or its consequences. Many a wandering sheep is oblivious to the damaging effects of a quickly overheard conversation or a half-truth misinterpreted or an event out of context. The good Christian shepherd has a special calling in the flock to be a "reality factor" for his people and to call them to examine what they themselves are quickly accepting. The perspective that a levelheaded deacon or minister can add to an uninformed church member is a healing force among the communion of believers.

A more subtle and debilitating influence in the local congregation is the seduction of the angry/manipulative person's behavior. By seductive I do not necessarily mean sexual seduction, but emotional seduction. Church members may at times express their anger and resentment in a very manipulative way by emotionally draining a pastor or staff member. Such deceptive exercises occur where persons have learned to express their anger indirectly, again, but with the additional dimension that they lean heavily on pastoral support until they have exhausted the minister's patience or emotional stamina.

Some persons make themselves emotionally dependent upon caring persons as a gesture of resentment. They often want to be fathered or mothered by someone who will make few demands upon them; they also become very angry that they depend on such emotional support from the pastor and resent either his strength or his gullibility.

Angry/seductive people need primarily a balanced ministry in which they receive just enough support to function on their own and gain personal confidence. The pastor who assumes a ministry with emotionally angry/seductive persons needs to assume and understand that he will be resented and rejected, loved and appreciated in alternating waves.

Some ministers have difficulty understanding the approach-avoidance signals that go on inside the angry/seductive person. Such church members want emotional support very badly; they also resent very much needing such support. Accordingly, whoever offers them support will be blessed one day and cursed the other. To ignore such feelings from parishioners and to move on with a steady, unwavering concern that is not "sucked in" either by inappropriate requests for nurture, or by extreme reactions of anger, is a helpful course of action.

A ministry with those who test and manipulate regularly requires a sense of security and confidence on the minister's part. Seductive parishioners need to be taken seriously but not literally. The emotional seduction may be verbal, in that the pastor may be told one day that this person "just simply doesn't know what they would do without him." That very same struggling friend may next accuse the pastor of not caring, of "being just like everyone else," and of simply "not living up to his calling." Such trying and shifting behavior is very much akin to the adolescent pattern of responses. The best ministry to these people is to be an unwavering, stable, and assured person of God.

One helpful internal signal I use to detect emotional seduction is the extent to which I dwell on that person's life or problem. If I think about a parishioner every once in a while (in prayer or concern), I am being appropriate with my feelings. If I dwell very frequently on that person, our conversation, how they are doing, what I could do more—I have become emotionally involved enough that I am vulnerable to emotional seduction.

Another aid in my ministry with the angry/seductive is to assess from time to time how much I am doing for other people. Jesus Christ was in the business of making people whole, of setting them free, and of helping them stand on their own two feet. To the extent that I work instead of the church member doing the work on their struggle, I am contributing to his problem. What I am doing is perpetuating his dependency, fostering his increased anger and self-hate, and crippling his own spiritual walk. Again, the caring pastor needs frequently to ask himself the question, Whose needs are being met with my actions? and What is the purpose of my involvement? Only by honestly assessing his own feelings and needs can the man of God protect himself from emotional (and sexual) seduction.

We have already suggested that firmness and directness are the best instruments in the healing of manipulation. Jesus was very direct with the mother of the sons of Zebedee (Matt. 20:20) when she and they wished to seduce him in choosing them to sit at his right and left in the kingdom. Notice how the remaining ten became angry over the issue. Perhaps each of them had aspired to such prominence, as we all do.

Paul is another good example of firmness and love. In Acts 15 several young Christians tried to manipulate Paul into "blessing" circumcision and rejecting Gentiles. They undoubtedly were motivated by a desire to undermine Paul's leadership and place him in an awkward spot; they underestimated his power and influence given by the Spirit of God. His firmness won the day (and the Gentile world) for Christ.

Aside from resisting manipulation and seduction, the pastor can respond in a constructive way to the church member who employs such deceptive tactics. The first good news the alert Christian will receive from the minister's resistance is that the representative of God will not be manipulated. Many angry persons who employ manipulation are relieved to discover someone they cannot push around. They often gain respect for such firmness and may, in fact, begin to rely on it as a safe mooring from which they can themselves begin to resist manipulative techniques.

Of course, many indirect and deceptive persons have learned to express their anger in such ways because any other way has only been too painful. For such persons to change approach or tactic requires a patient reinforcement of direct and open communication as rewarding. Few people dare take the risk of directness, especially if their early lives were immersed in painful experiences related to openness.

Sometimes the pastor can, over a number of years, become the faithful friend who does not abandon them or reject them and who receives their feelings without punishing them for having them. The main struggle with such indirect Christians is their own acknowledgement of such feelings, and in this ministry small progress is great gain.

Behind the need to manipulate is often the fear and anger that an individual nurtures about his ability to influence others. Many habitual deceivers seriously question their own competence around others and most often are overachievers with low self-esteem. They wish so desperately to count for something, and fearing impotence in all areas of living, they resort to manipulation as their only perceived way to achieve what they want.

Such anger at feeling inferior to others is rarely conscious or acknowledged. The angry/deceptive overcompensate for their personal fears by pretending overcompetence. They secretly despise those against whom they move for being more competent or able than themselves (as they see). Rarely do they know their own potential!

In such situations, a caring ministry involves both a firmness with the person and a steady affirmation of his strengths. The individual who recognizes some of his unfound gifts and abilities can begin to flex his own muscles in open and celebrative ways. He can soon, with confidence and genuine love, begin to cast away the works of deception which are no longer necessary tools in his quest for recognition. He can rise up, unafraid of his relative importance compared to others, and move beyond the anger of resenting other people's strength. He can, in fact, celebrate his own strength and affirm his own opinions openly.

All this is possible, but I am afraid it is also infrequent. Most manipulative church members I know are so ingrained in their patterns of behavior that they cause themselves to be feared by other members. Such avoidance breeds further anger, and the vicious cycle of anger/manipulation takes on more intensity. Only by the grace of God can a ministry of love and resistance, affirmation and control, confidence and firmness win over. And the Spirit of God is the key dimension to an atmosphere of such unique proportions.

The most important link, however, in a ministry with those who show their anger through manipulation is to help them understand that their indirectness is unnecessary. The open pastor can foster an atmosphere in which even those who have feared directness can venture to trust him or people in the congregation with their burdens of resentment. They will only do so in the steady evidence that such feelings are not going to be held against them. They need the assurance that their feelings will not destroy them or be rejected.

Behind much human manipulation is the mistrust of people. The shepherd of God needs realistically to understand that some persons have been taught for years that they cannot rely on people to openly move in responsible ways. They may not ever change such outlook, and caring ministers need not require of themselves that they change such long-established prejudices. A few manipulative people do change, but many never alter their manner of relating.

One final comment needs to be made with regard to the anger behind such deceptive behavior. Church members who adopt manipulation as a regular approach to people are usually confessing that they also have a low opinion of people and their ability to seek truth unhelped. My experience with such Christians (and with my own temptation to manipulate) is that at times we toy with the idolatry of believing that there is only one way for things to be done and that our way is *it*. Accordingly, we employ all possible indirect ways of influencing people toward our position—convinced that such manipulation is justified in order to arrive at the right solution.

A firm ministry with such misinformed Christians, then, is by necessity a persistent resistance to their covert overtures and work. God, from the beginning, limited himself by giving man human freedom and in so doing affirmed the possibility that his creatures could choose wisely—that he would not resort to manipulation to achieve his will. He is for us the model of openness and creative freedom; we become through his Spirit the enablers of such freedom by resisting those who forget to trust others with the same freedom they have been given.

A caring, patient ministry with the manipulative will often create a sense of distance rather than closeness and comfort for them. Pastor and deacon engaged in such shepherding must be prepared to expect that a regular consequence of resisting manipulation means possible rejection, cautious distance, or awkwardness. Some church members cannot handle being resisted while manipulating and will reject the pastor and his attempts. Sometimes minister or friend will even be accused in such cases of not being strong enough, of not doing his duty, and bowing out to what they know is right. Other times, particularly when manipulation is effectively resisted, the church member involved will become far more cautious or distant with the pastor.

Such space between manipulator and resistor is a declaration by the angry/manipulative that he recognizes an individual who will not put up with deception or half-truths. It is an acknowledgement of respect and should not be construed as a negative occurrence. It is, in fact, a sign that the inappropriate indirect behavior is being checked by the person himself.

The angry/manipulative need to know that they are accepted by ministering friends. Too much affirmation or assurance at this point is both misleading and confusing to such persons, who usually translate such overtures as either weakness on a minister's part or recognize it as a dose of their own deception. The pastor who cares, can, on the other hand, communicate directly and briefly from time to time with such church members in such a manner as to communicate that he continues to care. His gift of a polite distance offers the church member room to avoid too much interfacing—which is often awkward for him.

The angry/manipulative are not easy to become friends with, and the shepherd of the flock will probably discover that few people can relate to such persons and retain their own personhood intact. The angry/manipulative thus create a good bit of loneliness for themselves and hurt even more because of such isolation. A skilled pastor may need to disarm them from believing at such times that their isolation is a result of their unique integrity but more a function of their overwhelming control over relationships. Being direct with such persons is sound.

The manipulative can use even the pastor's good intentions against him. A wise ministry with such members means that at times (for example, when crucial conversations are being exchanged) minister and church member need to have their conversation confirmed by a third party (a deacon). That again was Jesus' advice to those who were facing relationship trouble (Matt. 18:16). If properly interpreted, the presence of the third party can be seen by the member as protection for himself as well as the pastor.

The Spirit of God is the only source of sufficient patience, forgiveness, and grace to minister to such difficult, hurting Christians.

8

The Care of Anger as Withdrawal

Sometimes the experience of alienation has taught us to back out and pull away from conflict. Some good Christian models resort to withdrawal as their way of coping with frustration and anger. Hampered by feelings they both dislike and fear, these committed people choose to detach themselves from individuals or congregations under the impact of strained relationships.

Most Christians have only seen damage and hurt when anger appears in a relationship, and the withdrawing church member has good intentions in his behavior. He is concerned that the pain and destructive power of anger not affect an entire congregation; he wants to take the impact of negative feelings out of the local church, so that it may explode more harmlessly, away from the crowd. He takes the anger then, with him, like a time bomb that is carried outside the body to explode with less damage.

Unfortunately, the church is the loser in such noble action. A significant leader has become incapacitated. In my study of alienated church members (people who had led active lives in local congregations, then left the local church under circumstances of disaffection), I found that only approximately one in four found his way back into another local church. And among those who did return

125

to church participation, only a small proportion became active and involved again.

What such behavior suggests is that most people who carry the anger of a negative personal experience tend to carry such feelings for a long time—tend to have difficulty letting go of their destructive baggage. What so many of these unhappy former church members described, as I heard them out, was an arrested state of emotions in which they remained incapacitated and unable to move on to new and constructive church involvements. They had not worked through their anger, and most often quite unconciously harbored unexamined and unfinished feelings that prevented them from reinvesting themselves in other churches.

Such members had frequently developed a distant and more apathetic attitude toward the local church. They had ignored their feelings, and, in the process, had pretended that such deep resentments simply would disappear. The harbored feelings had, again, become a barrier in their effectively relating to new Christian friends and new churches.

Our church roles are sprinkled with names of individuals who are supposedly only inactive and casually related to our congregations. A caring investigation of them will, I believe, reveal that many of them are actually angry, alienated church members who found, only in physical withdrawal, a solution to their painful feelings. Many such persons are deeply unsettled and hungry for healthy, Christian fellowship. They are torn between temporary relief, hurt, and loneliness. Some of them feel guilty over the distance they have adopted from the church; others feel a sense of peace over not having to contend with their feelings openly on a daily basis. All, I believe, are unsettled and incomplete in their resolution of their relationships to the church body.

To suggest that all inactive, withdrawn members are alienated people is to oversimplify the complexity of dynamics in church participation. In my study of disaffected and angry church members who had withdrawn from church participation, I discovered other shapes of withdrawal that bear some brief explanation in order to assist the minister committed to a healing venture among the withdrawn.

Some people who leave the church do so because of their particular stage of personal needs. The motive or incentive for church participation may, for example, no longer be present. Some families I met in my study had become involved in the church primarily out of a desire to involve their children in Bible study; once the children had grown and left, there was no longer the drive to attend or to remain active in the congregation.

Other members grow old together in a given congregation and have a sub-fellowship of believers within the local church which is "church" for them for many years. As this small circle of Christian friends begins to dissolve (by death, by moving, or physical impairment), such members lose their incentive for participation and begin to withdraw more and more. They feel that "their" church is dying and, in their eyes, that is so.

There are other participants in church who tend to relate to the local congregations very much like the nomadic farmer or migrant worker. They enter a congregation, deeply involve themselves rather quickly, and then pull out quickly—often from overexposure. They have a pat-

tern of overcommitment and move in and out of congregations in a cyclical pattern over months or years. I myself
know of several families who live under what I call the
"military time clock." Like the military family which is
geared to move every three years, to pull up roots and
move to the next place, these persons begin to feel restless
after a period of time and soon begin withdrawal symptoms.

Some church members exercise physical withdrawal as
the only method they know to curb overcommitment. They
count on pulling out of a local congregation after a period
of time in order to protect themselves from more involvement. Some persons, of course, use this pattern of "church
hopping" as a way of avoiding intimate relationships and
durable commitments. They move around in order to ease
the burden that close fellowship and continuity require.

Other one-time church activitists pull away from the
local congregation over grief and bereavement events. The
death of a spouse or close loved one, the occasion of a
divorce, or a major accident can become the precipitating
factor in a quiet, but usually temporary, withdrawal from
church participation. To push such people into premature
activity with the church again is often to ignore the deep
valley of feelings and the grief process through which they
are moving. Supportive contact from the church membership may be far more important than pressure to have
such members return to active duty very quickly.

Another factor in church membership inactivity is the
development of some moral dilemma in the life of a member. Active church members have explained to me (after
the development of trust) that they have moved away
from church activity because of such experiences as alco-

holism in the family, extramarital sexual involvements, drug usage, irresponsible business transactions, perceived failure in parenting, divorce, and so on. Such people judge or consider themselves unworhty of further participation in church and quietly withdraw with their private pain.

Such variety of reasons for withdrawal from church participation means that any program to reenlist inactive church members must take careful stock of the circumstances involved in the disengagement. To reclaim inactive church members requires a willingness to discover the shape of the interruption, its causes, and, where applicable, the road to a healing in the experience.

A ministry to those who have withdrawn from the church under circumstances of alienation will often encounter one of the following common experiences in churches: anger over being used by the church or a member, anger with a particular member (perhaps the pastor), disaffection over the direction or program of the church, and alienation over perceived neglect/offense.

Some churches have the insensitive habit of taking a talented church member and/or family and using their gifts indiscriminately without regard for such members' feelings or fatigue. Many a church has been a poor steward of members' talents by neglecting the biblical principle of a sabbatical in the life of an individual. Discovering talent and willingness in a member, some congregations abuse his gifts by using them to the point of exhaustion and overcommitment.

Some of our finest church members suffer from overexposure and burn-out in the local church. Apparently neither they nor the eager leadership of the church have learned to assess the limits of a person's commitments.

The result is often a guilt-filled withdrawal from church participation in order to regain one's energy and perspective.

Some members will often be criticized and misunderstood for such temporary withdrawal. Other members will talk about them, wonder about their commitment, or, even worse, pull away from fellowship with them. Feeling misunderstood and rejected, they frequently react by making permanent their action of withdrawal.

A few overworked Christians look around them and notice how little some of their brothers and sisters are doing in supporting the church effort. They become bitter and feel used by these less involved members. Soon the heavily committed member perceives himself as abused by less responsible or less involved churchgoers and decides to quit his load and pull back.

George was a young Christian whose conversion and early experience in the church was welcomed by all. He became the prize new member as the congregation celebrated his commitment and zeal. Inspired by their favor and support, he accepted several positions of responsibility and soon found himself the director of the Sunday School in his mid-size church. Elected twice to that responsibility, he began to sense that the membership at large was more eager for him to lead the congregational work than to participate with him in the various areas of teaching and administration. At first puzzled and disappointed by persistent refusal from members to assist him, he soon became an angry member who felt that his church was using him in the process of acclaiming his talents.

After three years of intense leadership in several organizations of the church, George communicated to the nominating committee of his church that he was not available for the next year's leadership responsibilities, and that he was going to spend more time with his family. He gradually began to spend more time at work and at home, becoming less involved in the services of the church. By the summer he was totally absent from congregational worship and participation.

George's condition was aggravated by a membership that did not know what to say to him in the face of this behavior. They felt awkward about any comments, and George interpreted their silence and lack of initiative as lack of care for him. He soon vowed that he would never return to that congregation regardless of subsequent overtures.

When I visited George, he had been absent from his home church for over a year and a half. He told me that he had visited one or two churches since his withdrawal but that somehow he had never moved with his family to transfer his membership and become involved again. He was a very lonely man, half wishing for the fellowship he had experienced at his first church, half wishing he could unite with some other vital fellowship. And in between the two options, he harbored unfinished resentment at his "first Christian family."

Several fine Christian leaders like George may be found in any local community. They agonize over a long relationship with their local fellowship which is now severed. A few such persons have expressed themselves too strongly in a public meeting (perhaps even held a reasonable point of view but carried it to an extreme). Others have primarily experienced a deep personality clash with the pastor or other leader in the congregation. Whatever the dynamics, most feel that they can never go back. The church, the individual, and the family of the individual are all losers in the event.

Is such withdrawal necessary? Is there an alternative to this painful detachment that leaves church and member depleted of vital talents? I firmly believe that a responsible investigation into each experience of withdrawal will offer ministers effective alternatives to Christian alienation.

Obviously, all such withdrawal will not be stopped. There is probably some withdrawal that is purposive and creative. There is also some detachment that will not be curtailed regardless of healing opportunities. But a great portion of angry/withdrawal can be redirected toward healing solutions where such reconciliation is desired and sought. It is to this end that the committed Christian minister can turn his energy and time.

Some preventive measures by the local congregation will do a great deal in anticipating a second cause of angry withdrawal: perceived neglect. We mention a few that we have found effective in our ministry. Others certainly are to be added, and pastors who have "sat at the feet" of the alienated can speak to ministries and attitudes they have found effective.

One suggestion (already alluded to) is that the church leadership in a local congregation be sensitive to and alert to the stewardship of time and energy among its members. Perhaps the committee most in position to oversee this ministry is the nominating committee of a congregation. Such a committee needs to evaluate the involvement of the members in various positions and responsibilities. The length of time a member serves and how many different demands are placed upon him is very important. Nominating committees should also determine what quality of cooperation a member is getting in his area of service, coordinating with Christian education and the pastoral leadership on potential areas of stress and miscommunication.

One creative possibility for a committee and minister is to bless individuals who need a rest with permission to take one. A tactful committee can approach an individual who is showing signs of wear in his assigned ministry. They can caringly inquire about the burden and joy the service he is performing brings; they can then assess whether the member would benefit from a leave of absence from his post. To suggest that a person's gifts are important enough that the church should never abuse them is a good way of introducing such a possibility.

A Christian of long service in any given area should be approached very carefully at this point. Many congregations have developed, by their neglect of the active member, an atmosphere of ownership with regard to certain positions in the church. When such occasions arise, both church and member suffer. The member suffers because his gifts and energy are abused and because he is expected to continue a task without reprieve.

The church suffers in such situations because the rich variety of ways in which people serve is hindered when only one person keeps a position. A wise and caring congregation will regularly distribute the gifts of persons annually. Such a careful stewardship of persons and time should never be arbitrary, but always in prayerful consideration of the needs of church and member.

I have several members on "leaves of absence" from our congregation from time to time. They are responsibly resting from a particular series of commitments in our church that have drained them. They are seeking Christian stimulation and renewal by visiting other congregations and by changing their patterns of service in the church. They are in regular conversation with me and other leaders in the church, keeping in touch and maintaining their perspective in the sojourn. They will return rested, challenged, and better equipped to be solid leaders in our congregation. They share from their pilgrimage of visitation new ideas and a deeper commitment to their faith; they enhance our church life by their excursion for us.

Other church members mainly need to sit it out one church year and absorb rather than give. The Christian life is one of give and take, and some of our potentially alienated members may just need a reprieve from their tasks in order to drink deeply of the well of Christian nurture. After all, isn't the Christian church designed to be a supply post of Christian strength and renewal for service in the world? The church then becomes the dynamic colleaguesmanship of individuals supporting one another.

Church members in need of rest need to be approached with sensitivity in regard to stepping down from their posts. Some members will readily see the need for the same and can even at times be assured of returning to their calling in that role. Others, unfortunately, are sometimes the last ones to notice the signs of wear and lessened effectiveness in their service. Like pastors who fail to see the need for a vacation in their ministry, such people need to be gently reminded that they hurt the congregation. Jesus Christ was the Master of work and rest; the Scriptures are replete with the symphony of his movement from crowd to desert. He engaged audiences and pressing crowds, then withdrew into the wilderness by himself. Sometimes he took his closest friends, but always he knew the hazard of ministry without interruption. I myself structure "minisabbaticals" from time to time with my congregation. They and I both benefit; they are blessed by the ministry and Christian outlook of a different preacher and pastor. I benefit by pulling away and gaining lost perspective, by retooling for ministry, and by renewal of commitment and vision.

A second preventive tool in a ministry with those who potentially may become estranged from their local congregation is one of initiative. By initiative I mean the sensitive, caring contact with a member of the church who recently was involved in some experience that could have produced misunderstanding or isolation. Pastor and deacon alike are able to discern at particular times that individuals in a public or private exchange may have developed hurt feelings. A follow-up on such an event can do much to prevent unnecessary alienation.

I find it rewarding and helpful to "check in" with members whose involvement in some decision of the church may have caused them pain. An invitation to lunch and a chance to chat on the subject gives the initiating pastor an opportunity to assess the extent of any hurt. Perhaps the pastor himself, again, is the focus of the hurt. A gesture of concern and interest (initiative) by pastor can begin the process of reconciliation.

Such initiative does not mean that two Christians need agree on a given issue. It means only that members of the body of Christ need not remain distant when differing in thoughts or belief. An indication by the pastor that he understands and accepts the member in such circumstances is good news and often alleviates the tension in a relationship.

Such contact also may determine if there have been some hurt feelings in a given circumstance (a third cause of alienation/withdrawal). Church members who have been offended by someone most often quietly bow out from exposure rather than express themselves. If they are given the opportunity to do so with pastor or offending party, they can manage their feelings without carrying them to inappropriate places (or the wrong party).

Sometimes members appreciate any awareness of their load by pastor or another church member. They may be in a position to continue their responsibilities; what they need is some care and appreciation in the midst of a heavy commitment. A regular visitation or contact ministry with the leadership of committees in the church is a good preventive gesture on the road to anticipating disaffection.

The pastor and church leadership are themselves in a position to foster an atmosphere in the church for openness and expression of feelings. Such a climate produces trust, minimizes friction, and encourages communication. Some of the alienation among church members is rooted primarily in lack of communication and understanding.

Having said and done all the above as much as possible, the average pastor (and most of us are) will need to accept the inevitability of some conflict and withdrawal in any congregation. It would be inaccurate to describe all anger and withdrawal as unhealthy in a church setting. One such example of a creative withdrawal was Walter.

Walter was a self-described liberal spokesman for a minority in a local congregation. He represented well the views of a few people who were deeply concerned about the conservative direction the congregation was taking. Over the years his pastor initiated conversations with Walter to assess his concern and support him as an individual. Walter subtly communicated his sense of frustration with the congregation over their perceived doctrinal position; he also conveyed a sense of isolation from the body and at times would lose perspective over his own feelings in the situation.

During a period of four years, several of Walter's friends and colleagues in outlook moved out of town. Gradually there were fewer persons exercising a support system for Walter in his frustration. He felt more and more at odds with newcomers in the church, since by his perception they seemed to espouse the conservative point of view he most decried.

Walter was a man of integrity and commitment. Twice he considered leaving the congregation, but his sense of responsibility and a deep fellowship tie with a small group in the church kept him from making such a decision. His frustration, however, intensified over the ensuing months, and heavier responsibilities at home and at work finally made his church relationship unbearable. By the time he came to the pastor with a renewal of his struggle, his mind was made up.

He did not ask the pastor for support when he called to see him. He came to indicate that he had prayed about and carefully evaluated his current relationship with the church and that he had decided he was leaving. He did not hold the congregation to blame for a deep sense of alienation he felt from them; he confessed to a different theological outlook than the majority and described his frustration as significant enough that further fellowship was hampered.

The pastor received his announcement with seriousness and care. The man was not one to make quick, rash decisions. So the minister received his decision in the spirit of openness with which it had been offered, acknowledged the differences which Walter was feeling, and accepted his verdict as a responsible and caring decision. He explained to this devoted church member that he was not going to argue with him over his decision to withdraw out of respect for the member's careful and serious consideration of the matter.

He went on to indicate how much the member and his family had contributed to the fellowship and balance of that church. He stated how sorely he would be missed. Then he went on to trace some plan of action that would supportively and lovingly assist this church member as he disengaged from his present fellowship and sought another.

Walter did not need pleading or cajoling. He had made up his mind. The pastor knew his situation by having kept in touch with him. He did need (and deserve) affirmation. The minister was appropriate in expressing his personal sense of loss (since he felt it); if the feelings were not sincere, the member would have known it. The pastor eased the pain of this member's conflict with the church by not arguing with him about it.

This church member's family needed support and care during their transition from one fellowship to another. To transfer fellowship from one congregation to another need not be in a spirit of rancor. Pastors and members can and should work supportively to help make this family's pilgrimage a more meaningful one. Any personal sense of rejection should be secondary consideration in such circumstances.

The above pastor helped Walter consider one or two congregations where he might find the particular quality of fellowship and theological outlook he required. When churches and ministers work together in this fashion, competitive feelings are dismissed. Nor did Walter feel slighted or pushed out by his present pastor; he understood him enough to know that he was trying to minimize the parishioner's pain, ease the transition, and affirm the variety of Christian churches through which the Spirit of God works.

Congregations and churches need to be regularly educated to the meaning of church membership and the significance of affiliation. The people of God need to understand the complex factors at work in human associations; the most important goal to strive for in church participation is the harmonious work of a people who find enough fellowship to overcome their differences and participate in a constructive, basically unified direction. When people come to a place where they find their relationship to a congregation impairing their Christian experience of fellowship, they need to search for a different group with whom they feel compatible enough to fellowship.

Angry church members who withdraw need to be visited when they have done so. For all the above reasons, there is no way for pastor or deacon to know why a member disaffiliates. The fear of offending by inquiring into the cause of a separation is overshadowed by the possibility that the church member may already be offended and much in need of understanding or reconciliation. In human relationships, guessing what happened is always inferior to finding out what happened. How can those who care for people care effectively if they have no idea of what to care for?

If the "physician of the soul" is to exercise any healing influence in a member's life, he should know something about the nature of the withdrawal situation. Church members who create distance do so for a reason; the caring pastor will investigate and learn from the experience. Only those who are already offended may react in offense, but those who do usually have decided to react in offense prior even to a gesture by the minister of God.

We have mentioned elsewhere the significance of reconciling individuals who have offended one another in the body. The pastor can again act as a mediator in a conversation between persons who fear they will either lose control or actually fear confrontation with another. The mediating pastor will want some assurance from both parties involved in a "summit meeting" that they are open to a constructive resolution of any conflict.

There is little value in gathering two offended persons together only to see them vent their frustrations and destructive comments on each other. A healing attitude must be present on both sides for a possibility of understanding and Christian communication to exist.

What about the member who withdraws out of differences with the pastor? The deacon or other caring member here exercises a significant ministry of intercession for the pastor. In consultation with the minister (and every pastor should expect some members to be unable to relate to him), this caring friend can be the one to determine if such differences are reconcilable. He can faithfully interpret the pastor's point of view, listen to the grieved member, and bring the grace of God to bear on a relationship in such a way that the member can evaluate more accù rately whether or not he can further "be member" with his pastor.

Some members will decide that they cannot continue to serve with a particular pastor or person. They can be gently supported as they seek another church fellowship. The deacon or other caring persons can help minimize the conflict that can occur in such disengagements, for he himself can be the sustaining assurance of trust for both parties in such conflict. He can assist the pastor in coming to terms with his finitude (he cannot minister to everyone effectively), and he can aid the withdrawing member to discover the need to reengage with another fellowship without having to vent destructive feelings in a manner that will require intensive "pastoral first aid" among the membership.

Particular issues and decisions by the church can also bring about the physical withdrawal of a faithful member. Initiative to that person is first in order, and a committed attempt to discover exactly what the issue is will be of importance. The possibilities of reconciliation and compromise then become a first calling. As we have stated elsewhere, the gathering of two or three in Christ's name can do a lot to bring together those of different mind who may continue to respect one another's point of view in an atmosphere of acceptance where differences can be aired.

But there are also occasions where a deep sense of differences occur, and no reconciliation is possible. Paul and Barnabas found it necessary to go separate ways in a second missionary effort after they had exchanged points of view. God used both parties in that situation, and the people of God need to remember that he has enough work for all to do in his kingdom. When differences become major factors among Christians in a small fellowship, each has to evaluate his continued commitment to that group.

A member may choose to leave a congregation over some issues, and his leaving need not be decried as destructive. There are occasions when a member clearly senses that his position and that of the body is clearly divergent. He may then exercise God's will in retaining the sense of unity of the fellowship by withdrawing himself. His stewardship and outlook can effectively be used by God in another place and perhaps more effectively be channeled by another congregation. Pastor and caring leaders sometimes need to bless this departure as inspired by God. Prayerful and careful evaluation of the circumstance will help determine if such is God's will.

Above all experiences of anger as withdrawal, the Spirit of God needs to be invoked as constant mediator in differences, a reconciler in distances, and a guide in new commitments. God has frequently used even the angry withdrawal by a member (sometimes a caring gesture, as we shall note yet) as a means through which he multiplies his body and achieves new unity of purpose.

9

An Ongoing Ministry with the Angered

The previous pages have attempted to identify different shapes of anger in the church for purposes of effective ministry. The various expressions of alienation mentioned certainly do not cover all the manifestations of anger in the church. Our hope is that by discussing certain aspects of anger in the church we might be able to more effectively minister to people in our congregations. The primary assumptions we have made are that anger itself is neither constructive nor destructive, that it frequently occurs among committed Christians, and that many people have poor models for a constructive expression of anger.

A lingering illusion may be that all anger is resolved by proper management. Such an unwarranted conclusion would deny the evidence that Christians who become angry often do so for some very important reasons and that their anger may just as often be clarified but not dismissed. There are, in fact, as we have stated at the onset, some very appropriate and justified reasons for anger. Christian anger can be an expression of care, a resistance to abuse, a reaction to manipulation, and righteous indignation at a wrong. Perhaps a word about each of these legitimate responses is next in order.

Some relationships warrant a degree of commitment and trust between persons that elicit genuine anger when

deficient. Deeply committed Christian friends may sometimes react in appropriate anger to someone who treats
their friendship casually or with insensitivity. I recently
listened for several hours to an individual who felt slighted
and taken lightly by another person. The one in question
had broken a confidence by passing on information to a
third party which had been given in clear secrecy to her
by the first person. The church member very responsibly
confronted the friend with the breach of integrity, dis-
closed her feelings of anger, and withdrew to compose
herself.

When these two friends came to see me they were both
obviously in a great deal of emotional pain. Each was
suggesting that the other did not care for them; both felt
hurt and angry. I suggested to them that they consider
their anger in the following light: (1) the first person (I
suggested) was angry with her friend because she cared
very deeply for the relationship and did not want to lose
the trust established; (2) the second was very angry at
being found out and being confronted with the issue.

Both persons were finding it easier to allow alienation
to separate them than to deal with the pain in the relationship. I affirmed the first member's feeling of anger as appropriate and as a genuine affirmation of the quality of
relationship she was expecting from her friend. Behind
her anger was a caring request to be taken more seriously.
She also was willing to take her friend seriously enough
that she would not pretend the issue had not occurred
and then quietly remain angered with her for months to
come.

Some people don't care enough about one another to
deal with their differences and move beyond them. They

prefer to live in the agony of private anger rather than handle the pain of vulnerability and clarity. They are the losers in their choices.

Confrontation and evaluations of this kind require God's forgiveness for a relationship to survive. All who exercise this caring anger and forgiveness report to me that their relationships have reached new dimensions of commitment. Evidently a mature expression of caring anger can be the occasion for deeper Christian friendship.

Some persons who make themselves available to assist and help others become prey to abuse. Some very gentle and generous people I know in congregations will occasionally be exploited by others who will abuse their goodwill. Such people will often wait a long while before they acknowledge being used but then will even surprise themselves with the amount of resentment they feel over such behavior.

Christian anger is an appropriate expression in the face of abuse. God himself in the Bible most often expressed his anger at Israel for this cause: the people exploited his generosity and grace to the point of ridicule, and he declared an end to their misuse of his love. So church members at times need to declare their best efforts as victimized and their sincerity and willingness as exploited.

The Christian who manifests angry feelings on such occasions is often using the only emotion an exploitative or abusing friend will hear. Regardless of whether he is heard, his angry reaction contributes at least in two ways: (1) he declares a stop to the abusing behavior and (2) he honestly and therapeutically expresses strong feelings that need venting to the offending party.

Other Christians practice a significant ministry of control when they vent anger over being manipulated by others. The extractive or manipulative person will sometimes only be curtailed in his attempts by the firmness of someone who will not allow that person to further use him or someone else. By declaring the behavior openly, the confronting Christian also "flushes out" any subsequent manipulation and warns the schemers in our churches that such subterfuges will be exposed.

Perceptive Christians are called in congregations to protect their less sensitive brothers by declaring a halt to manipulation wherever they see it. Church members have the right to express anger at manipulation and abuse, both against themselves and their brothers. Jesus Christ was regularly manifesting his anger at the Pharisees and Sadducees for their manipulative and deceptive practices among the Israelites. Christ saw his weaker brother's vulnerability to exploitation and made it his business to challenge such behavior with deep emotion—appropriate anger.

There are instances where a public or private wrong elicits authentic anger. I have seen committed Christians rise up in righteous indignation over the atrocities of a Nazi regime, the dehumanization of a black, or the prejudice of an immature church member. Christians sometimes reach outstanding witness by a proper sense of anguish and revulsion at the destructive attitudes and actions of other human beings.

As painful as confrontation sometimes is to both parties involved, Jesus Christ himself employed such means to communicate his beliefs and feelings. He spoke in anger at Pharisees whose prejudice made them far more concerned about rules than little people; he reviled religious groups for becoming so pious that they ostracized and rejected others. He dared to call some people "white-washed tombs," with an implication that what was inside was very rotten. He did it in righteous anger, and I believe Christians also exercise that spirit appropriately.

I remember, for instance, the brother who sat at a meeting and heard several members explain why they could not receive a certain group of underprivileged children on the church premises. He listened patiently for a few minutes to each argument against the projected ministry, then suddenly rose in indignation and confronted his best friends: "The truth of the matter is that we do not want them here because we are prejudiced!" he stated.

Many people felt uncomfortable that evening, and a few felt weighed and found at fault. And the open expression of anger by a member who loved his friends enough to state the truth in their faces was a Christian gesture of ethical responsibility.

Christian love at times requires anger as its full expression of concern. Such anger should never be confused with destructive emotions which actually wish the worst. Perhaps the best evaluation of our anger is to ask ourselves whether with it we still wish the good and the helpful to prevail or if we are primarily concerned with retribution, vindictiveness, or hate.

The question of continued forgiveness in the face of a wrong is of concern to the Christian. How many times shall an individual be alienated by the repetition of inappropriate or irresponsible behavior—and still be open to reconciliation? The interpretive tradition of the Hebrews suggested that since God forgave three times, (Amos 1:3,6,9) the believer was released from forgiveness by the fourth occurrence. Peter (Matt. 18:22) surpasses even rabbinic expectations when he inquires of Jesus if seven forgiven wrongs should be the limit, only to be told unequivocally that the limits for a believer were limitless ("until seventy times seven").

The New Testament teachings of Christ seem to confirm this perennial attitude of forgiveness on the believer's part (Luke 17:3-4, probably in a different context). Continuous forgiveness as a Christian attitude in the face of wrong is certainly the functional model of the Christ, who even from a painful cross reaches out with the staggering words: "Father, forgive them, for they know not what they do" (Luke 23:34), in speaking of a crowd who, though misguided, was committed to his death.

Experience informs me that most of us, in the face of continued wrong, need forgiveness for an inability to forgive. Unlike the Master, we reach the end of our rope, and like the popular western hero whom we worship for avenging all wrongs, we draw the line and declare that we shall take no more. Our pride is colored by our sense of feeling used in a process of repetition which confesses that the abuser is not learning from his behavior. We suspect that there is lack of sincerity in such repetitive injury; we question whether we are in fact contributing to the forgiven person's problem by allowing him the freedom from the consequences of his acts.

Only a clear conscience and a sense of the Spirit's presence can evaluate at which point the Christian will abandon his stance of forgiveness. Regardless of how others have acted, the churchman in leadership is called to remember that the God whom he worships had many occasions to quit forgiving a very undeserving people. Somehow he never allowed pride to dim his vision for forgiveness, even though he faced the toughest of fickleness and callous disregard.

Obviously the church member or minister involved in repetitive occurrences of a wrong will need God's patience and a supportive ministry from others. He may need to back away from the demands of forgiveness by chronic abusers. He may need to exercise God's wisdom of judgment whereby he delays forgiveness as a "purging wait" for a casual abuser. After all, Israel was constantly forgiven by God but not always without a forty-year wilderness or a four-hundred year exile.

The shepherds of God are called to be discriminating guides among the flock. They must help his sheep discern between "the spirits of destruction" and of God. We all walk together in the wisdom of the Spirit which is our only hope of properly guiding the stewardship of anger in our midst. The task is delicate, for there is much distorted history in our personal lives with regard to anger. Yet, by the Spirit of God and under his constant grace, the ministers and people of God can become together the caretakers of one of God's most unique emotions.

Anger, in the prayerful hands of the people of God, can rise to be the channel of concern, commitment, and love that it deserves in the church. And by the grace of God, with patience and Christian sensitivity, anger can become primarily a constructive force for the expression of ethical concern, personal commitment, and corporate action. After all, has not history shown us that some of the most important steps in the lives of nations and people have occurred only when they have become angry enough at some wrong that they have determined to invest themselves in its redeeming counterpart?

The preceding pages have been an effort to assist the people of God in their pilgrimage with anger. The intention has been that a clarification on the various expressions of anger in the church might more effectively assist ministers and shepherds in the caring of the people of God "on the way." The remaining hope is that all who read this offering may invoke the guidance and presence of the Spirit of God. He is the essential ingredient in the recipe for a continuous healing of anger in his church, that the people who call themselves by his name may become, in fact, the redeemed and redemptive family of God!

10667340

Kylie Jean

Cooking Queen

by Marci Peschke

illustrated by Tuesday Mourning

PICTURE WINDOW BOOKS
a capstone imprint

Kylie Jean is published by Picture Window Books

A Capstone Imprint

1710 Roe Crest Drive

North Mankato, Minnesota 56003

www.mycapstone.com

Library of Congress Cataloging-in-Publication Data

Cataloging-in-Publication information is on file with the Library of Congress.

Names: Peschke, Marci, author. | Mourning, Tuesday, illustrator.

Title: Cooking Queen

ISBN 978-1-4795-9899-1 (library binding)

ISBN 978-1-4795-9901-1 (paper over board)

ISBN 978-1-4795-9905-9 (eBook PDF)

Creative Director: *Nathan Gassman*

Graphic Designer: *Sarah Bennett*

Editor: *Shelly Lyons*

Production Specialist: *Laura Manthe*

Design Element Credit:
Shutterstock: blue67design, kosmofish

Printed and bound in the United States of America.
010368F17

For the true cooking queen, KJH, and
two little bakers — Maxie and Gwen
— MP

Table of Contents

All About Me, Kylie Jean!

My name is Kylie Jean Carter. I live in a big, sunny, yellow house on Peachtree Lane in Jacksonville, Texas, with Momma, Daddy, and my two brothers, T.J. and Ugly Brother.

T.J. is my older brother, and Ugly Brother is . . . well . . . he's really a dog. Don't you go telling him he is a dog. Okay? I mean it. He thinks he is a real true person.

He is a black-and-white bulldog. His front looks like his back, all smashed in. His face is all droopy like he's sad, but he's not.

His two front teeth stick out, and his tongue hangs down. (Now you know why his name is Ugly Brother.)

Everyone I love to the moon and back lives in Jacksonville. Nanny, Pa, Granny, Pappy, my aunts, my uncles, and my cousins all live here. I'm extra lucky, because I can see all of them any time I want to!

My momma says I'm pretty. She says I have eyes as blue as the summer sky and a smile as sweet as an angel. (Momma says pretty is as pretty does. That means being nice to the old folks, taking care of little animals, and respecting my momma and daddy.)

But I'm pretty on the outside and on the inside. My hair is long, brown, and curly.

I wear it in a ponytail sometimes, but my absolute most favorite is when Momma pulls it back in a princess style on special days.

I just gave you a little hint about my big dream. Ever since I was a bitty baby I have wanted to be an honest-to-goodness beauty queen. I even know the wave. It's side to side, nice and slow, with a dazzling smile. I practice all the time, because everybody knows beauty queens need to have a perfect wave.

I'm Kylie Jean, and I'm going to be a beauty queen. Just you wait and see!

Chapter One
Picking Pecans

On Saturday morning when Ugly Brother and I wake up, it's cold. It's finally sweatshirt weather! The air in my room is chilly. I snuggle under the covers. Sometimes it takes a long time for fall to come to Texas.

I look over at Ugly Brother. He is snuggled at the end of my bed. "Do you know it's almost Thanksgiving?" I ask.

He barks, "Ruff, ruff."

Two barks — that's a yes! Then again, maybe he's just barking because he heard me say *Thanksgiving*. Ugly Brother loves turkey so much. Drumsticks are his favorite!

"Don't get too excited. It's still three weeks away," I tell him.

Finally, I scoot out of bed. I pull on my jeans and sweatshirt. Ugly Brother barely moves.

"Come on, lazy bones!" I call. "You can't stay in bed all day. Today we're picking pecans so I can make my famous pecan pie for Sunday dinner."

Ugly Brother tucks his face between his paws, looking disappointed. But then the smell of bacon wafts up from the kitchen downstairs. It distracts him. He bolts from the bed and starts to scamper, and I quickly follow.

If we were racing
to the breakfast table,
Ugly Brother would
win. By the time I get
to the kitchen, he's
standing next to my
chair with a piece of

bacon hanging out of his mouth. It looks just like
a tongue.

"Someone sure loves bacon!" I say.

Momma turns to look at Ugly Brother, and we
both laugh. Then she puts more bacon in the big
black skillet. She makes eggs and toast too.

Daddy and T.J. come in, and we all eat
breakfast together. Everyone talks about our
Saturday plans.

* * *

It's a nice brisk fall day, so Momma and I
decide to take Ugly Brother on a walk to Pecan
Park to pick pecans after breakfast. Our route
takes us past our neighbor Miss Clarabelle's house.
We wave as we pass.

Miss Clarabelle waves back from her rocking chair. Her porch is dotted with pumpkins of all shapes and sizes. She even has the big flat round pumpkins that look like Cinderella's carriage. People call them Cinderella pumpkins.

"Isn't Miss Clarabelle's porch pretty?" I say. "I just love her Cinderella pumpkins! They remind me of princesses, and princesses make me think about queens. You know how much I love queens!"

"Those Cinderella pumpkins are so short and squatty," says Momma. "I like the traditional orange ones that didn't get cut for Halloween."

Momma has Ugly Brother on a leash so he won't run away. Momma and I each have a big brown paper sack with handles to hold the pecans we will gather.

We are enjoying the colorful leaves and
the beautiful fall day. It's still early as we walk
through town. On our way to the park, we see
shop owners starting to switch their signs from
closed to *open*.

When we pass the Harvest Food Pantry, I notice
they have a giant sign in the window. It says *Feed
a Needy Family for the Holidays.*

"Look, Momma," I say. "What does the sign
mean, exactly?"

"We have so many good things to eat, Kylie
Jean," says Momma. "Some people are less
fortunate, and they go hungry. We should fill
a bag at the grocery store to donate to the food
pantry."

I nod my head. For the rest of the walk, I'm quiet. I'm thinking that there has to be a way to help lots of hungry families. If I had a lot of money, I'd buy a truck full of groceries for them.

When we get to the park, Momma says, "You're awful quiet, sugar. Are you ready to pick pecans?"

"I'm thinking about something important," I tell her. "Since we're already at the park, I'm going to pick pecans and think at the same time!"

Momma and I decide to have a race to see who can get the most pecans. We spread out under the tall trees and begin to fill our bags. I'm thinking I have an advantage since Momma has to hold the doggie leash and pick up pecans. Plus Ugly Brother keeps trying to get into her bag and eat the pecans!

Momma and I
both laugh at our
silly doggie, because
these nuts are still in
the shell. This year
there's a good pecan
crop, so it's easy to fill
our bags. The nuts in
my bag get closer and
closer to the top.

"I'm done!" Momma calls to me. "My bag is
filled to the brim."

"Yay, Momma!" I shout.

Momma walks over to me. She looks in my bag.
It's almost full. "Yay, Kylie Jean!" she says.

"Well, I think we have enough pecans," I say.

"We sure do!" replies Momma. "Let's head back home, sugar."

Momma tugs on the doggie leash, and we set out for home. Ugly Brother is slow. I think he's tired! Momma and I pass the Harvest Food Pantry again. I'm still working on a plan to get a truck full of food for those hungry folks.

Soon we are back home. Momma preheats the oven for my famous pecan pie. The secret is in my crust. The recipe was my great-grandmother's. Everyone called her Maw.

Momma and I wash our hands and put on our aprons. Together we measure out the ingredients for the crust.

I put the flour in the bowl. Momma adds the shortening. I add a pinch of salt. We use a kitchen tool called a pastry cutter to mix the dough together. We know it's ready when the dough looks like a bowl full of little white peas. The last thing we do is add several tablespoons of ice water. And then we mix it all together with a fork. I gently pat the dough into a ball.

Next, I sprinkle flour on the counter under the ball of dough. I roll out the dough with my wooden rolling pin. Then I use Momma's trick. Very carefully, I roll the circle of dough over the edge of the rolling pin. Then I move the dough into the pie pan. Momma cuts off the extra dough, and I crimp the edges with a fork.

"You are quite the baker, little lady," says Momma. "Now let's make the filling."

"Yes, ma'am," I reply. "Can we put the leftover dough on a pan with some cinnamon sugar too?"

"Of course!" Momma tells me.

We make the filling by placing corn syrup and butter into the mixing bowl. Then we add sugar, eggs, salt, and vanilla. Once it's all mixed, we add the pecans. Momma pours the filling into the crust. Then she pops it into the oven.

When the pie is finished baking, we put it on the table to cool. A mouth-watering, brown sugary, caramel perfume fills the air.

Daddy says, "I'm ready for some of that delicious pie!"

T.J. says, "Me too!"

"No one is eating any of this pie," Momma says. "It's for the potluck at Nanny's house tomorrow."

Potluck dinners are the best because everyone brings a dish to share. Usually Nanny makes Sunday dinner. But Momma and Aunt Susie think it might be nice to give her a break. Plus, my cousin Lucy will be there tomorrow. I can't wait to see her!

Maw's Pie Crust

Ingredients

- 2 ¼ cups all-purpose flour
- ⅓ cup butter-flavored shortening
- ⅓ cup regular shortening
- 5–8 tablespoons of ice cold water
- pinch of salt

Instructions

1. Chill shortening for 30 minutes.

2. Stir flour and salt together in a deep bowl. Using a pastry blender, cut the shortening into the flour until the dry ingredients form pea-sized crumbs.

3. Using a fork, stir in 1 tablespoon of ice water at a time until a dough ball forms.

4. Roll out on a floured surface. Put dough in pie pan. Trim and crimp edges. Now you are ready for pie filling!

Chapter Two
Potluck Party

On Sunday morning before church, Momma and I make French toast for breakfast.

"You are really enjoying cooking this weekend," says Momma.

"I like to cook all the time!" I tell her.

I crack the eggs with a *tap, tap, tap* on the edge of the bowl. Then I pour in the milk. Next, I swirl in the vanilla and sugar. Finally, I add a dash of cinnamon. I use a metal whisk to stir the mixture.

"Momma, are you going to help me dip the bread in the egg mixture and flip it onto the skillet?" I ask.

She replies, "I will if you find T.J. and Daddy to set the table."

"You've got a deal!" I say.

T.J. comes in just in time to put the plates on the table. He's tall, so it's easier for him to get them out of the cupboard anyway.

Daddy comes in last. He passes the skillet to T.J. to place on the table. Then he grabs a small piece and stuffs it into his mouth. He smiles and winks at Momma.

"My compliments to the chef," Daddy says. "This breakfast is delicious!"

"Kylie Jean is the chef this morning! And you should wait until you get to the table to eat your food," Momma tells him.

Daddy winks at me.

T.J. nudges Daddy. "Hey, I put the plates on the table," he says.

"Great!" replies Daddy. "And next weekend you and I can cook breakfast."

Momma smiles, and we all start eating our breakfast. Soon Momma looks up at the kitchen clock, and then she jumps up out of her chair.

"Oh, no! We're going to be late for church!" she cries as she grabs her purse.

We all jump up and run around. Daddy grabs the keys. T.J. grabs his jacket. I run for the door.

I almost forget the pie for the potluck dinner at Nanny's house. We're going there straight from church. But thankfully Ugly Brother reminds me by barking in the kitchen.

* * *

Later at Nanny's, the table is piled high with food. There's fried chicken, veggies, desserts, and my special pecan pie too. We all get plates and form a line to dish up. The kids get to go first, then grown-ups, and finally Nanny and Pa. They are the hosts, so they get their plates last. Nanny says it's just good manners to let your guests go first.

When everyone has a plate, Pa says the blessing. Then we all dig in! At first, it's so quiet you could hear a pin drop. Momma says if people aren't talking, it means the food is really tasty.

My best cousin Lucy is sitting right beside me. She leans in toward me. "I don't like to bake much," she whispers, "but I know you do. Your pie is delicious!"

"Cooking is one of my favorite things," I tell her. "Actually, I love cooking almost as much as I love queens and the color pink."

Lucy gasps. "Well, I can't believe it!" she replies. "I thought you'd never love anything as much as you love pink!"

"Momma won all sorts of cooking ribbons at the county fair. I guess she just passed that love of cooking on to me," I explain.

Lucy nods. When we are done, we take our plates to the kitchen. Then we ask if we can go play outside.

Nanny says, "Just for a while. Today, the grandkids wash all of the dishes."

Last weekend, the kids washed them. By the kids, I mean Momma, Daddy, and all the aunts and uncles. It's funny to think of them actually being kids!

On our way to the barn, Lucy and I see most of the grown-ups settled into the den. They're watching the Cowboys play. Daddy says Sunday afternoon football watching should be a requirement.

Lucy and I play tag. I'm only *it* once, but Lucy gets tagged several times. I would say Lucy is a slow runner, but I know she's not.

"Lucy, are you trying to get caught?" I ask her.

Lucy laughs. "Maybe . . . I like being *it* and chasing you around. Then I don't have to worry about getting tagged."

Just then, Nanny calls us in to do the dishes. Momma and Aunt Susie are in the kitchen with Lilly and T.J. Everyone is raving about my pie. Lucy and I get dish towels. We are always part of the dish-drying crew.

I see Momma and Aunt Susie talking quietly in the corner. I think they're up to something because Momma looks a little sick, like she just swallowed a June bug.

She asks Nanny, "Mom, can we have Thanksgiving at my house this year?"

We all look at Nanny and wait for her answer. Now Nanny is the one who looks like she swallowed a June bug!

"It's just that the family has gotten so big, and hosting Thanksgiving dinner will be a lot of work for you," Momma adds.

Nanny asks, "Shelley, are you sure you want to take on this big holiday meal?"

"I am!" says Momma.

Nanny finally nods. "Well, if you're sure, I guess we can try it this year." She seems a little sad. I think she likes cooking for a big bunch.

Aunt Susie is still going on and on about my yummy pie. "Did you hear about that cooking contest for kids on the *Good Morning, Texas* TV show?" she asks.

"No, ma'am," I tell her.

"Shelley, you just have to help Kylie Jean enter that contest," Aunt Susie says.

Momma says, "Kylie Jean can cook a lot of different dishes. I'll check into that contest."

* * *

On the way home, Momma and I have a little chat. "Momma, do really think I could enter that cooking contest and be a cooking queen?" I ask. "It sounds fun!"

"Of course you could," says Momma.

"Will you help me enter?" I ask her.

"Sure, sugar!" she says. "I bet we can find out by looking on the Internet. We'll do it this week."

I found out two exciting things today. First, I found out we are having Thanksgiving at our house this year. Second, I'm going to try and enter that cooking contest. I hope there's a prize! Maybe I can use it to buy food for the Harvest Food Pantry.

Cinnamon French Toast
Serves 4

Ingredients

- 1 egg
- 1 teaspoon vanilla
- ½ teaspoon cinnamon
- ¼ cup buttermilk
- 1 tablespoon light brown sugar
- 4 slices bread

Instructions

1. Beat egg, vanilla, brown sugar, and cinnamon in shallow dish. Stir in milk.

2. Dip bread in egg mixture, turning to coat both sides evenly.

3. Cook bread slices on lightly greased nonstick griddle or skillet on medium heat until browned on both sides.

4. Dust with powdered sugar or serve with maple syrup.

Chapter Three
Official Entry

The following night, Momma helps me look up the contest on the Internet. The website says kids who want to enter need to make a video entry. So Tuesday evening, I try to pick out an apron to wear for my video entry for the *Good Morning, Texas* Kids Cooking Contest. Momma laid out several aprons on my bed, and Ugly Brother wants to help me too.

"I need this apron to show the TV station that I am a real true kid chef! If I win, I will be able to do something very important," I tell Ugly Brother.

"I'll be able to help the Harvest Food Pantry!"
I twirl around, showing him my pink cupcake
apron. "Do you like this one?"

Ugly Brother barks, "Ruff." That means no.

I guess he isn't a fan of pink cupcake aprons. Too bad I love pink!

"I bet you'd like a bacon apron!" I joke.

He barks excitedly, "Ruff, ruff! Ruff, ruff!" Then he chases his tail in a circle.

I study all my options. The apron I wear for the contest needs to be special. For a while, I consider Momma's lucky blue-and-white checked apron. I even try it on. She has worn it to every state fair cooking competition, and she always wins.

"I really want to be picked for the contest because I'm good at cooking, not because I'm wearing Momma's lucky apron," I tell him. "Do you know what I mean, Ugly Brother?"

"Ruff, ruff," he barks.

I decide to stick with my pink cupcake apron instead. I run downstairs to show Momma.

"That one is perfect, sugar," Momma says.

Just then, T.J. comes in the back door. He has agreed to help me make my audition video. "Ready to make a movie, Lil' Bit?" he asks.

I nod. Ugly Brother moves close to me so I won't feel nervous. Momma told me that a friendly face will make filming easier. Every time I get nervous, I'm going to think of Ugly Brother with that piece of bacon hanging out of his mouth!

"My video has to have two parts," I tell T.J. "I have to say how long I've been cooking and why I think I should win. Then I have to cook a main dish. I'm making my special pizza. It's one of the only main dishes I know how to make."

"Okay," says T.J. "Let's get started!"

"Can we do the cooking part first?" I ask.

"Sure!" he replies as he picks up his phone to start filming.

While T.J. films me in the kitchen, I get all my ingredients and place them on a cookie sheet. I learned from Momma that a neat kitchen helps a chef make a good dish. I will use crescent rolls for my dough. They're easy peasy! I preheat my oven, and then I press the rolls out in one big piece on a baking sheet.

My nerves still have me feeling a little jumpy inside, but then I see Momma and Ugly Brother watching me. I think about his bacon tongue, and I want to laugh out loud!

Next, I mix softened cream cheese, sour cream, and herbs in a small bowl. When I hear the oven beep, I know it's time to put the crust in and set the timer.

"I'll help you with that, sugar," Momma says as she places the crust in the oven.

"Thanks, Momma," I say.

Next, it's time to slice the vegetables with my tiny chef's knife. Momma watches me closely. She has taught me how to use a knife the proper way.

First, I put the onions in cold water. Then I carefully cut them into rings. Momma taught me that special trick so my eyes won't tear up. Next I slice the mushrooms.

Finally, it's time for the peppers. I have a special plan for them. I'm going to julienne them! That means I'll cut them into thin, shiny green ribbons that are all the same size. This trick should make the TV folks really happy. I hope they'll think I have super chef skills!

The oven timer goes off, and Momma pulls out the crust I made. "Wow, look at that gorgeous golden color!" she says.

Now that the crust is cooked, I spread on the cream cheese topping, making a creamy sauce. Then I add the veggies. The pizza looks beautiful!

T.J. looks impressed. He pauses the video to say, "That looks amazing, Lil' Bit!"

I smile and hold the pizza up so he can get a good shot. Then I begin talking to the camera. "Hey, y'all! I've been cooking for as long as I can remember," I say. "I started out with my pink play kitchen when I was an itty-bitty baby! I think I should win because I am creative, and I put a lot of love into my cooking."

Momma smiles and gives me a thumbs-up.

I continue my speech. "Now, I just bet you thought I was going to make a regular pizza, but I didn't! Using the freshest ingredients is very important to me. I spend a lot of time on a farm. And we get a lot of farm-fresh food to cook up and serve on our table. Fresh food tastes delicious! I sure wish y'all could try this — it's so good!"

Ugly Brother is drooling at my feet. I know
because I feel a puddle forming there, but I don't
let it distract me!

I smile and take a big bite of pizza. "Yummy!"
I exclaim.

"Cut!" says T.J.

"You were perfect, sugar!" says Momma.

"Thanks, Momma," I reply.

Momma and T.J. both step in for a piece of my
pizza. I even sneak Ugly Brother a little piece while
we watch the finished video. We all agree it turned
out pretty good.

Later that day, I cross my fingers as I e-mail
my cooking video with help from Momma. Now I
have to wait to hear if I am chosen for the contest!

Easy Veggie Pizza Pie
Serves 8

Ingredients

- 2 8-oz. cans refrigerated crescent dinner rolls
- ½ cup sour cream
- 8 oz. cream cheese
- 1 tablespoon herb seasoning
- ½ cup each green bell pepper, mushrooms, and red onion

Instructions:

1. Heat oven to 375°F.

2. Unroll both cans of crescent roll dough; separate dough into 4 long rectangles. In an ungreased 15 x 10 x 1-inch pan, press into bottom and up sides to form crust.

3. Bake 13–17 minutes or until golden brown. Cool completely, about 30 minutes.

4. In a small bowl, mix cream cheese, sour cream, and herbs until smooth. Spread over crust. Top with vegetables. Serve immediately.

Chapter Four
Filling the Pantry

On Thursday after school, Momma and I go to the grocery store. I have a grocery list for my busy baking weekend. But I also have a secret mission.

"How was school?" Momma asks as we drive.

"Fine," I reply. "Lucy and I got to work on a science experiment together."

"That sounds exciting," she says.

I shrug.

"Are you feeling okay, sugar?" asks Momma.

"Yes, ma'am," I reply.

When we get to the Piggly Wiggly, they have a poster in the window that says *Harvest Food Pantry: Feed a Hungry Family for the Holidays*. I guess the Piggy Wiggly already knew all about my secret mission!

Inside, I get one of those little shopping carts for kids. Momma gets a big cart, and we start down the first aisle. Momma loads up on canned veggies. I do the same!

Momma looks surprised. "What kind of dessert has green beans in it?" she asks.

"Remember when we went to pick pecans? You said we could fill a bag for the food pantry the next time we went to the store," I remind her.

"I've had a lot on my mind, but yes, I do remember now," Momma replies. "I'm so glad you reminded me!"

Momma helps me pick out corn bread mix, cans of pumpkin, and cranberry sauce. We also grab other food staples like flour, sugar, and shortening. Soon my tiny cart is overflowing!

Momma laughs. "I think we have more than one bag of groceries in your cart," she says.

"Can we drop them off at the pantry on our way home?" I ask.

"Sure, sugar," Momma replies.

We finish shopping and check out.

"We're getting food for the food pantry," I tell the cashier.

"That's wonderful," she says. "I'm proud of you for wanting to help. In fact, I think I may buy some food for the food pantry too. You have inspired me!"

I smile a big smile. That makes me feel really good! "Thanks," I tell her. "I'm happy to help."

Momma and I grab our bags and head to the parking lot. We load up the back of the van with our bags. Then we head downtown to drop off our food at the pantry.

Momma parks the van. "We'll have to drop these bags and go. We have our own groceries in the van too," she says.

"Okay, Momma," I reply.

We pick up the bags of food for donation from the back of the van and walk inside. The pantry is bright and cheerful. The walls are painted a soft yellow. Shelves filled with food items line the walls. But some of the shelves are empty. Just then, I see my neighbor Miss Clarabelle!

"Miss Clarabelle!" I shout. "Are you giving food to the pantry too?"

"Not today, dear," she says. "Today is my day to volunteer here at the pantry."

"What does a volunteer do?" I ask.

"Well, I stock the shelves, and I help families fill their sacks," she tells us. "But sometimes the shelves don't have enough food. That means we have to turn hungry families away."

"I see some empty shelves," I say. "It looks like the pantry needs more food!"

Miss Clarabelle nods as she unpacks our grocery bags. When she's done, she smiles and gives me a big squeezy hug.

"Thank you!" she says. "You've done a great job shopping, Kylie Jean. We hardly ever have cans of pumpkin here. The families will really enjoy some of these special Thanksgiving treats."

"I've got a plan to get more food too," I tell her. "Just you wait and see . . . "

* * *

Later that evening, Nanny comes over. She has something covered in clear plastic wrap in her arms. She hands it to Momma, who carefully unwraps it. Inside is the giant family turkey platter.

"I guess it's time for the next generation to take over cooking for the holidays," Nanny says. "So I am passing the platter to you, Shelley."

"Thanks, Mom. I hope I will do a good job feeding the family for Thanksgiving," replies Momma.

Momma and Nanny sit at the kitchen table talking about favorite family recipes. Nanny still looks a little sad. T.J. doesn't notice because Nanny has loaded the platter with her famous butterscotch oatmeal cookies. Momma doesn't seem to notice either. She's busy asking Nanny questions.

"Will all of the family members who live in Jacksonville make it for Thanksgiving this year?" Momma asks Nanny.

"Yes, it will be a very large group this year!" replies Nanny.

Momma turns toward me. "Kylie Jean, can you please get a pen and my notepad from my desk?"

"Yes, ma'am," I reply. I run upstairs and grab Momma's notebook and pen. Then I quickly head back down to the kitchen. I want to help Momma with the Thanksgiving meal.

"Thanks, sugar," Momma says.

"You're welcome," I tell her. "Can I help?"

"Of course," she says.

Nanny smiles and pats the chair next to her. I slide into it. Together, Momma, Nanny, and I make a list of everyone who will be coming to our Thanksgiving feast.

> Guest List for Turkey Day
>
> Aunt Susie and family–5
> Nanny and Pa–2
> Granny and Pappy–2
> Louisiana cousins–5
> Arkansas cousins–3
> Miss Clarabelle–1
> Our family–4

That makes a total of 22 guests! And Nanny keeps on thinking of other things that Momma needs to do.

Nanny looks over at T.J. He's still huddled near the turkey tray. "T.J., slow down, or there won't be any cookies left for anyone else," she tells him.

T.J. frowns and sets down a cookie.

"I'm going to be testing out recipes all weekend for the contest," I tell Nanny. "I'm making trail mix, double chocolate crispy rice treats, and chocolate cupcakes with caramel filling and fudge frosting. I promise to bring something extra tasty to Sunday dinner!"

"It's going to be a double-chocolate weekend!" replies Nanny. "Well, it's getting late, so I'll be heading home. I'm looking forward to seeing which of those delicious treats you're going to bring to Sunday dinner!"

Before she leaves, Nanny passes out hugs and kisses to everyone. Then Momma says it's time to do homework and get ready for bed.

Butterscotch Oatmeal Cookies

Makes 24 cookies

Ingredients

- 1 stick softened butter (½ cup)
- 1 cup dark brown sugar
- 1 egg
- ½ teaspoon vanilla
- 1 teaspoon baking powder
- ½ teaspoon cinnamon (optional)

- ½ teaspoon kosher salt
- 1 cup all-purpose flour plus an additional 2 tablespoons
- 1 cup butterscotch chips
- 1 ½ cups rolled oats

Instructions

1. Preheat oven to 350°F.
2. In a large bowl with a hand mixer or the bowl of a stand mixer, cream together the butter and brown sugar.
3. Add the egg and mix until incorporated. Add the vanilla, baking powder, and salt. Mix until incorporated.
4. Stir in the flour, then stir in the butterscotch chips and rolled oats just until combined. Mixing too much will create tough and dry cookies.
5. Drop rounded mounds of dough (about 2 tablespoons each) onto ungreased cookie sheets. Press down dough mounds slightly with the back of a large spoon before baking.
6. Bake until just lightly browned on the edges and the middle still looks undercooked, about 9 minutes.

Chapter Five
Chef Kylie Jean

Over the weekend, I impressed my family with some super-chocolatey cupcakes! All day Monday at school, though, I can't stop thinking about the *Good Morning, Texas* cooking contest. I just can't wait to find out if the judges liked my video!

When I get home, Momma has something exciting to show me. I have mail! I drop my backpack and run to the box on the kitchen table. It's a very special package from KTRE, the local TV station.

"Momma, this is it!" I shout.

"I've been waiting all day!" Momma cries. "Hurry and open it!"

I rip the brown paper from the box. Ugly Brother helps. I pull the flap open. The box is filled with tissue paper and colorful confetti!

"This is so exciting!" I gush.

I dig through the confetti. The box seems empty, so I hold it up and shake it. A white envelope falls to the floor from its hiding place in the box. Ugly Brother brings it to me and lays it at my feet. It's a letter with the competition rules.

"Come sit at the table and we'll read the letter together," says Momma.

We both pull up a chair. Excitedly, I read the letter out loud.

Dear Kid Chef Contestant,

You made it! We loved your video entry, and we want you to compete in the *Good Morning, Texas* Kids Cooking Contest. Congratulations!

Rules:

There will be three rounds at our studio: snack, main dish, and dessert. A fully-stocked pantry will be provided.

Each kid chef may bring only an adult sous chef to the studio.

Judges will be TV host Joe Conrad, culinary professor Kathy Lane, and local chef and restaurant owner Amy Roberts.

Kid chefs should report to the KTRE studio on Saturday, November 19th for preliminary rounds. The final round will be on live TV at the studio Monday, November 21st. Again, congratulations and good luck!

The winning kid chef will receive a $100 check.

Sincerely,
Amber Jones, Producer

Momma says, "I've been to Amy Roberts' restaurant, Amy's Bistro, and the food is really delicious."

"Can we go there before the contest?" I ask.

"Let's go tonight to celebrate!" Momma says.

"Yay!" I cry.

Ugly Brother barks and runs around the kitchen. He thinks he's going too!

"No dogs allowed at the bistro," says Momma.

Ugly Brother whines. I know he's sad.

"Don't worry," I tell him, "I'll bring you my leftovers in a doggie bag.

I run upstairs to change clothes. I put on a pink dress with a little sparkly sweater. I brush my hair and put a big pink bow in it. While I'm changing, Daddy and T.J. come home. Momma tells them the plan. By the time I get back downstairs, everyone is ready to go.

The bistro is right downtown. On the big glass windows, it says *Amy's Bistro* in fancy black letters. Daddy holds the door open for us.

Inside, the tables have white tablecloths and cloth napkins. Chandeliers twinkle above us, and candles glow on the tables.

"This bistro is so fancy," I exclaim. "I love it!"

Momma says, "Just wait until you taste the food. It's delicious!"

"I'm ready to eat anytime," replies T.J.

We all laugh. The hostess leads us to a table and gives each of us a menu. Our server comes right over to fill our crystal glasses with ice water.

"Should we order a starter?" Daddy asks.

"Let's try the bruschetta," Momma tells him.

Momma has made bruschetta at home before. It's like toast, but it has tomatoes and fresh basil on top. It's delicious!

Everyone is looking over the menu.

T.J. says, "I'm having the steak."

"Me too," says Daddy.

"I'm having something fancy — chicken cordon bleu," I tell them.

"Me too!" Momma says.

Our server takes our order. Before long, the starter is served. Everyone agrees it is delicious!

"Will we see Amy Roberts tonight?" I ask.

"Let's ask our server if she is here," says Daddy.

When the server brings the main dishes, Daddy asks if Chef Amy is cooking tonight. But the server tells us Chef Amy is away at a special event. Her sous chef is cooking tonight instead.

Everyone digs in. My chicken tastes amazing! It has ham and cheese stuffed inside.

Eating such a tasty main dish reminds me that I have a problem. I need to make a main dish other than my pizza to win the contest and become a cooking queen. I really want to win the one-hundred-dollar prize. I know that money could buy a lot of food for hungry families.

I'm not very good at cooking main dishes, but I know just who to call for help!

Tomato Basil Bruschetta
Serves 6–10

Ingredients

- 1 loaf French bread, sliced
- 6 cherry tomatoes, diced
- 8 fresh basil leaves, cut into ribbons
- 2 tablespoons of Italian dressing
- ¼ cup of extra virgin olive oil
- salt and pepper to taste

Instructions

1. Preheat oven to 450°F.
2. Dice the tomatoes, then mix with dressing.
3. Wash and cut basil into narrow ribbons.
4. Brush sliced bread with olive oil. Bake on a foil-wrapped cookie sheet for 5–7 minutes.
5. Top warm toast with tomato mixture and basil.

Chapter Six
Main-Dish Misery

On Tuesday afternoon, in the middle of our messy kitchen, I ask if I can call Nanny. I really need her help with my main dish. Nanny is an amazing cook.

Momma says, "Yes, you can call Nanny. I'm sorry, but I am way too busy practicing new Thanksgiving recipes to help you!"

"Do you want me to stay here and help you, Momma?" I ask.

"No," she replies. "My plan is to try out these vegetable casseroles so I'll know if they'll work for Thanksgiving Day."

I call Nanny right away. *Ring . . . ring . . . ring!*

Nanny answers, "Lickskillet Farm . . . hello?"

"Hi, Nanny," I say. "It's Kylie Jean. I really need your help! Are you busy this afternoon?"

Nanny is not busy. She is very excited and heads right over to pick me up. On the way to the farm, I look over at Nanny.

"What is it, sugar?" asks Nanny.

"Nanny, will you please be my sous chef for the cooking contest this Saturday?" I ask.

"Yes, yes, yes!" she replies. "Being on your team would make me so happy and excited!"

At Lickskillet Farm, Nanny's kitchen is neat as a pin compared to Momma's. Before we start cooking, I put on my pink cupcake apron. Nanny puts on her checkered apron. Then she places some steak, chicken, and eggs on the kitchen counter.

"What kind of main dish can you make with steak?" Nanny asks.

I think for a few minutes, and then I reply, "How about grilled steak?"

"That's a great idea," Nanny agrees. "But to turn it into a winning idea, you will need to make your main dish extra special."

I see her point. Grilled steak is just steak.

"How about steak tacos?" says Nanny.

"That's a great idea!" I tell her. "Momma has been teaching me how to cook on a grill pan."

First, Nanny and I very carefully slice the steak into thin strips. Then we use a grill pan to cook the strips. We decide to add some other ingredients to our tacos too — sweet potatoes and fresh spinach.

"Nanny, what about the cheese?" I ask.

"How about Brie cheese? And let's use pesto for a sauce," says Nanny.

Pesto is made with olive oil and herbs or nuts. We make ours from pine nuts and basil from Nanny's garden. We crush it all up in the blender.

Next, we cook the chopped sweet potato in a skillet with a little olive oil. When it's almost soft, we add the spinach. The last thing I do is heat whole-wheat tortillas on a griddle.

After stuffing the tortillas and adding the
cheese, we taste them.

"These tacos are super yummy!" I say. "I'm
going to call them Farmhouse Tacos because the
ingredients are fresh from your farm!"

"I love these tacos, and I love you!" says Nanny. She gives me a big squeezy hug.

Just then, I hear Daddy's truck bumping down the dirt road.

"I love you too, Nanny!" I say. "Thanks for making me a main-dish superstar. Goodbye until Saturday!"

I blow her a kiss and head out the back door.

Farmhouse Steak Tacos

Ingredients

- 8 whole-wheat tortillas
- ½ pound skirt steak
- 4 oz. Brie cheese
- ½ bag rinsed fresh spinach
- 2 medium sweet potatoes
- 2 tablespoons olive oil
- ¼ cup pine nuts
- 1 small jar pesto (or make your own)
- salt and pepper

Instructions

1. Brush grill pan lightly with oil. Then place the pan on stovetop set to medium heat. Slice steak and add salt and pepper to taste. Cook until fully browned.

2. Dice sweet potato and cook in skillet with a tablespoon of oil. When almost cooked, stir in ½ bag of spinach.

3. Heat tortillas.

4. Assemble tacos by adding pesto, meat, sweet potato/spinach mix, and cheese. Top with pine nuts.

Chapter Seven
Good Morning Gourmet

On Saturday morning, I wake up when it's still as dark as the inside of a pocket. I don't want to be late! Ugly Brother is a big sleepyhead. He doesn't want to get up, but he watches me get ready. I put on my pink T-shirt and black pants.

Downstairs, Momma is also up early. She's waiting to braid my hair. I sit down in front of her, and she gives me some advice as she braids.

"If you get nervous, all you have to do is think of Ugly Brother cheering you on," she tells me. "Remember, Nanny will be there to help you as your sous chef. In fact, Nanny will be here any minute to pick you up. I wish I could go with you, but you can only take your sous chef. You've got this, Kylie Jean!"

"I really want to win, so I'll do my best!" I reply.

"Maybe this will help," Momma says. She holds up a pink ribbon with sparkly cupcakes on it. The ribbon looks just like my special apron!

"Momma, that's beautiful!" I cry. "Thanks so much."

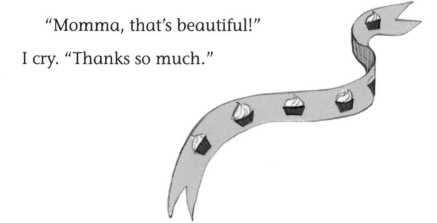

Momma ties the ribbon in my hair. "I have one for Nanny too," she says as she hands me a checkered headband.

"Nanny will love this," I tell her. "I'm going to surprise her with it!" I grab my pink cupcake apron and tuck the headband into a pocket.

Momma hands me a muffin and a glass of milk. I gobble up the muffin and chug down the milk. I finish just as Nanny arrives at the door.

"Ready?" she asks.

"Yup!" I shout.

Momma says, "Whoa, wait a minute! I want to give you a good-luck hug!"

She gives me a big squeezy hug. Nanny and I head out to the car and drive to the TV station.

Inside the studio, we have to sign in. We go straight to the desk in the lobby. A nice woman with *Mabel* on her name badge hands us a clipboard. At the top it says *Good Morning, Texas Kids Cooking Contest Contestants*. Down the side, it lists the names of all the kids and their sous chefs.

Once we're signed in, I put on my apron and tie it tight. Nanny puts hers on too.

"Nanny, I have a surprise for you," I tell her. "You can wear this too." I hand her the blue-and-white checkered headband.

"This is perfect!" says Nanny as she ties the headband around her head. "Thank you."

"Okay, then," says Mabel. "I'll just take you back to the studio."

We walk through a building bigger than my school. Mabel says there are a lot of sets at the station. There are some for morning programs, some for news, and some for specials.

The set for the morning show has been converted into a large kitchen. It has ten miniature cooking stations. Each one has a cooktop, an oven, and a small workspace. Each station also has a stool. I'm glad because I'm a bit too short to reach the cooking area. There is also a huge refrigerator and pantry area to use.

Mabel introduces us to Amber Jones, the producer.

"Nice to meet you, Miss Jones," I say.

"Just call me Amber," she replies. "Welcome to the set. There will be nine other kids from ages eight to twelve competing with you today."

Guess what? One of the other kids competing, whose name is Colton, says his dad is a real chef. He's also Colton's sous chef. I'm not worried, though. Nanny is a fantastic cook, and I have her!

It's time for round one. All of us kid chefs head to our stations with our sous chefs. Amber reads the rules out loud. I'm so excited, I feel as jumpy as a kernel of corn in a popcorn popper! We have just forty-five minutes to make a snack. I take a deep breath.

Amber counts down, "Ten, nine, eight, seven, six, five, four, three, two, one . . . the clock starts now!"

All the kid chefs and their assistants start running around like crazy! I grab a cookie sheet to hold all our ingredients.

"Great idea!" Nanny says.

"I learned this trick from Momma," I tell her.

Next, I grab oats, pumpkin seeds, maple syrup, pecans, and raisins. Then I get brown sugar, salt, dried cranberries, and white chocolate chips. I send Nanny to the refrigerator to get butter. My plan is to make a fall trail mix. I think the judges might enjoy the flavors.

Nanny preheats the oven while I put the pecans on a cookie sheet to toast them. Nanny waits for my signal to put them in. Finally, I hear the buzz that tells me the oven is preheated. I give Nanny the thumbs-up. She puts the pecans in, and I ask her to melt the butter in the microwave.

Next, I carefully measure out all of the dry ingredients into a bowl. I have memorized my recipe, which is good because I will only have a few minutes to mix my snack. We will need time to bake it in the oven.

Nanny comes back with the melted butter, and I stir it together with the salt, brown sugar, and maple syrup. Suddenly, I realize the pecans are still in the oven.

"Nanny, the pecans!" I shout.

Nanny runs over and pulls the pan out of the oven. "We got them out just in time!" she says.

The girl next to me named Gwen says, "I'm glad your pecans are okay. If they had burned, that would have been an awful setback."

"Me too! Thanks!" I reply.

I stir everything together and spread the pecans back out on the baking sheet. Nanny puts the pan back in the oven. When it is done and slightly cooled, we add white chocolate chips. We finish right before Amber calls time.

The judges for today are Amber and the camera crew. They try all the snacks. Some kids have made a meal, not a snack. Gwen put too much salt in her cheesy tater tots. I'm sad that she's out. She seemed so nice.

I'm nervous, but I want to jump for joy when Amber calls out the names of the kid chefs moving on to the next round. The five kids who are going to make a main dish are Colton, Maxie, Jake, Ashley, and me! For the next round, the main dish, we will have forty-five minutes.

When Amber calls time to start, I go straight for the steak. I ask Nanny to get the grill pan while I gather the rest of the ingredients. We both stay focused and cook, and our Farmhouse Steak Tacos turn out great!

Everyone presents his or her main dish. Colton has made a very delicious-looking pot of stew. I see Maxie's plate, and it looks beautiful. Ashley and Jake have made dishes that look really good too. How will the judges pick the finalists?

I see the judges taste all of the dishes, and they keep talking and looking at their clipboard notes. Then they taste my tacos and Colton's stew a second time. I'm so nervous! I try to think of Ugly Brother cheering me on.

Finally Amber says, "The two kid chefs cooking on live TV on Monday will be Kylie Jean Carter and Colton Brooks. Congratulations!"

Nanny and I jump up and down excitedly!

"We did it, we did it!" I cheer.

Nanny says, "Let's call your momma and tell her the good news!"

Now we have to wait until Monday for the final competition. Colton will have his dad for his sous chef again, but I will have Nanny! I give her a big squeezy hug.

"You're my secret good luck charm, Nanny!" I tell her.

Nanny smiles all the way home.

Pumpkin Trail Mix

Ingredients

- 3 cups rolled oats
- 1 cup dried cranberries
- ½ cup raisins
- ½ cup pumpkin seeds
- ½ cup pure maple syrup

- ½ cup toasted pecans
- ¼ cup brown sugar
- ¼ cup butter, melted
- ½ teaspoon salt
- 1 cup white chocolate chips

Instructions

1. Preheat oven to 300°F.

2. In a large bowl, stir to combine rolled oats, dried cranberries, and pumpkin seeds.

3. On a cookie sheet, toast pecans in oven for 3–5 minutes until they are shiny but not burned. Add to bowl of dry ingredients.

4. In a separate bowl, stir to combine maple syrup, brown sugar, melted butter, and salt. Pour wet ingredients over the oats and mix well.

5. Pour the trail mix onto a rimmed sheet pan and spread it out evenly with a spatula. Bake for 30 minutes, stirring halfway through the baking process.

6. Let the trail mix cool completely, and then add white chocolate chips. Store in an airtight container at room temperature for up to two weeks.

Chapter Eight
Bake Off

On Monday, Nanny and I need to head back to
the KTRE studio bright and early in the morning.
We will be competing in the dessert round of the
competition. Momma is wishing me good luck
when Daddy comes through the kitchen on his
way out the back door to work.

Daddy says, "Good luck, Lil' Bit. You're going
to be fantastic!"

"I hope so," I say. "This time Nanny and I are going to be on live TV. We are both as nervous as catfish in a hot skillet!"

Momma, T.J., and Ugly Brother are going to be watching us at home from the living room couch. Momma is going to record *Good Morning, Texas* so Daddy can watch us on TV when he gets home.

Nanny comes in as Daddy is leaving, and we all walk out together. It's a short drive to the TV station. At the studio, we sign in again with Miss Mabel. Colton and his dad are right behind us.

Mabel says, "You will be cooking in a different part of the studio this time."

Today we are on the actual set of *Good Morning, Texas*. This time everything looks the same, except there are only two work spaces.

There is also a big ice-cream maker. Across from us is another stage that has big chairs and a coffee table for the hosts of the morning program and the judges.

The hosts and the judges come over to introduce themselves. Joe Conrad is quiet, Kathy Lane is tall, and Amy Roberts is wearing a beautiful scarf. They all welcome us to the show. The camera crew waves and smiles. They all seem really nice.

Amber, the producer, explains the rules again. "This time, you have one hour to make your dessert course. Our hosts will introduce you, and then you can begin cooking."

I turn to Nanny and whisper, "There are a lot of really bright lights."

"Stay focused!" she says. "Once you start cooking, you won't even notice."

I try to think about Ugly Brother eating that bacon. It makes me smile.

One of the hosts, Vickie Baker, walks over as the show starts. She explains the contest again and welcomes us to the program. Then she asks each of us to introduce ourselves and our sous chefs. I go first.

"Good morning, Texas!" I say. "My name is Kylie Jean Carter, and I'm pleased as punch to be cooking for the judges today. This is Nanny, the best cook in Texas. If we win, we are giving all of our prize money to the Harvest Food Pantry. They feed hungry families."

Nanny looks surprised.

"Oh, and one more thing," I add. "They are taking bags of groceries. Just drop your bag off at their place downtown. Thank you for caring and for sharing!"

"That's very inspirational, Kylie Jean," Vickie Baker says. "Thank you, and good luck."

Next is Colton's introduction. "I'm Colton, and I love to cook!" he says. "This is my dad, and he is the best cook in the world."

"Good luck, Colton!" Vickie replies. "You two are already very competitive! Let's get started. Ready? Start cooking in three, two, one . . . go!"

Colton and I race to the ingredients table. I'm making my famous pecan pie because Aunt Susie told me it's a winner! I grab the pecans while Nanny goes to the refrigerator for butter and eggs. In the pantry, I grab sugar, vanilla, flour, salt, and corn syrup.

I also look for one more secret ingredient. I am thinking about what Nanny said about making my recipe special. I want to put chocolate in my pie. I look for baking chocolate bars, but Colton already took them.

Oh, no! A plain old pecan pie can never win this contest. Back at my station, I explain the situation to Nanny.

"Maybe he won't need all of the chocolate," she says. "Why don't you ask if you can have some?"

I head over to Colton's station. He is cooking something on top of the stove. I have to hurry, because my pie needs thirty minutes to bake.

"Can I please have some chocolate?" I ask.

Colton stops stirring the pot and says, "No, I'm sorry, but I'll need all of it for my ice cream."

I run back to my station and tell Nanny.

Nanny says, "We'll just do our best."

She turns on the oven while I make the piecrust, rolling it out with a big wooden rolling pin. Nanny puts the crust in the pie pan while I mix the filling. The whole time, I've been thinking about how I can make this dessert special.

Finally my pie is ready to go into the oven.

Nanny says, "Well, it looks beautiful. Let the chips fall where they may."

"Nanny, that's it!" I shout. "We can use chocolate chips instead of baking chocolate." I rush to the ingredients table and grab a bag.

When Nanny sees me sprinkle those chocolate chips all over the top of my pie, she winks at me. My pie will not be a plain old pecan pie. It will be special! We get it into the oven so it can bake.

We catch our breath for a minute. Then I realize Colton is making brownies with chocolate ice cream. It's a bake off! I decide that while my pie is in the oven, I'll make some homemade whipped cream since Colton is making ice cream!

The pie and brownies come out of the oven at almost the same time. I overhear the hosts saying they smell something delicious.

Colton and I both get our plates ready for the judges to taste. I slice my pie into a perfect wedge. Then I scoop a huge dollop of the whipped cream on top. It still looks a little plain, so I sprinkle some chocolate chips on top.

Stepping back to give my plate a final look, I think it is pretty fancy. It's perfect!

The judges taste the desserts. I watch their faces, but they seem to like both of our desserts. Vickie steps toward us with the microphone.

"Kylie Jean, can you tell us why you think you should win today?" she asks.

I turn to her and the camera. "I have a lot of experience!" I say. "My family is full of great cooks, and they've taught me everything they know. I think I should win because I put a lot of love and creativity into my food."

"Excellent!" she replies. "Colton, how about you?"

"I should win because I'm just the better cook," Colton says. "After all, I've had a professional chef as a teacher."

"Let's take a commercial break," Vickie announces. "When we return, we'll announce the winner of the *Good Morning, Texas* Kids Cooking Contest!"

The break only lasts a few minutes, but it feels like forever. The judges are still talking together, and soon the camera lights come back on. The show is starting again.

Vickie looks into the camera and says, "It was a very close contest. Both of our contestants should be so proud. Both desserts were absolutely delicious!"

Then Vickie Baker smiles and says, "In fact, they were so delicious the judges couldn't choose. We are calling the contest a tie!"

Nanny and I are surprised. We laugh and hug.

"You two will have to share the prize money," Vickie says. "Each of you will get fifty dollars."

Nanny and I walk right over to congratulate Colton and his dad. Vickie walks over too.

Colton shakes my hand. "I'd like to give you my money for the Harvest Food Pantry," he says.

"That's the nicest thing I've heard in a long time," Vickie says. "Kylie Jean wins, Colton wins, and the really big winner is the Harvest Food Pantry. If Kylie Jean and Colton can donate their winnings, I think the station can match their donations. Let's make it two hundred dollars for hungry families!"

Everyone in the studio cheers.

I go home with my chef coat, bragging rights as a real true cooking queen, and a full and happy heart! I can just imagine all the food we can buy for the food pantry. We might even be able to fill up the back of Daddy's pickup truck!

Chocolate Pecan Pie Filling
Serves 8

Ingredients

- 3 eggs
- 2/3 cup white sugar
- ½ teaspoon salt
- ⅓ cup butter, melted
- 1 cup light corn syrup
- 1 cup pecan halves
- 1 ½ cups chocolate chips
- pie shell

Instructions

1. Preheat oven to 375ºF.
2. Mix all ingredients together in a bowl and pour into prepared pie shell. Bake for 40 minutes.

Chapter Nine
We Are THANKFUL

Early on Thanksgiving Day, Momma gets up before Mr. Rooster even crows. She needs to get our big ol' turkey in the oven so it can cook. All day long, she is rushing around getting the rest of the cooking done.

Now that it is almost time for the meal, more people are here to help in the kitchen. Aunt Susie is helping, Lilly is helping, and Lucy is helping too! I am mashing potatoes with a big potato masher.

Lucy is standing next to me. "That looks hard," she says. "Good thing you're a cooking queen!"

"The trick is to mash them without squishing them out of the bowl!" I tell her.

Family members poke their heads in the kitchen as they arrive. "Hi, y'all!" they say. "Happy Turkey Day, and congratulations, Kylie Jean, cooking queen!"

"Thank you very much, and I hope y'all will try my prize-winning pie," I reply. "It has chocolate, and you know chocolate makes everything taste better!"

More and more people arrive. Dinner is not ready, pots and pans are piling up, and Momma's to-do list on the refrigerator is still full.

Momma goes straight to Nanny and gives her a big ol' squeezy hug. She says, "Maybe it's not time for you to quit cooking Thanksgiving dinner after all. Just look at this mess!"

Nanny smiles and says, "I just happen to have my apron in my purse!"

Lilly leaves to help T.J. and Daddy set up extra tables in the living room. Pa comes in to help in the kitchen. With Nanny giving the orders like a head chef, the food is ready in no time!

Lucy, Daddy, Lilly, and I carry big bowls of steaming hot food out to the serving table. Everyone has finally arrived. We all find a place at the table. Daddy carves the turkey. While we pass the dishes and load our plates, everyone takes turns saying what he or she is thankful for.

Momma says, "I am grateful that my mom is going to take back that turkey platter, because cooking Thanksgiving dinner is a huge job!"

Nanny says, "I'm thankful that I have my platter back, because cooking for this family makes me very happy!"

When it's my turn, I think about all the folks down at the food pantry. I'm so glad they will have food to eat today. I may be a cooking queen, but that's not what's really important. I look up at everyone around me and say, "I am thankful for all of the delicious food we have to eat and for my wonderful family!"

Leftover Turkey Sandwiches

Serves 6–10

Ingredients

- 2 slices of your favorite bread
- 2 slices of leftover Thanksgiving turkey
- 1 tablespoon of mayonnaise
- 1 tablespoon of cranberry relish
- 2 lettuce leaves, rinsed and dried

Instructions

1. Lay the pieces of bread on a plate or cutting board.
2. Spread the mayonnaise on one slice and the cranberry relish on the other.
3. Put turkey and lettuce on the cranberry relish slice and top with the bread that has the mayonnaise on it.
4. Cut in half diagonally.

Marci Bales Peschke was born in Indiana, grew up in Florida, and now lives in Texas with her husband, two children, and a cat named Cookie. She loves reading and watching movies.

When **Tuesday Mourning** was a little girl, she knew she wanted to be an artist when she grew up. Now, she is an illustrator who lives in Utah. She especially loves illustrating books for kids and teenagers. When she isn't illustrating, Tuesday loves spending time with her husband, who is an actor, and their two sons and one daughter.

Glossary

advantage (uhd-VAN-tij)—something that helps you or puts you ahead

competitive (kuhm-PET-i-tiv)—very eager to win, succeed, or excel

crimp (krimp)—to make wavy

distract (di-STRAKT)—to draw the attention away from something

inspire (in-SPIRE)—to fill someone with an emotion, an idea, or an attitude

producer (pruh-DOOS-ur)—a person who is in charge of making a TV program

rave (RAYV)—to praise something enthusiastically

scamper (SKAM-pur)—to run lightly and quickly

setback (SET-bak)—a problem that delays you or keeps you from making progress

1. Kylie Jean celebrates Thanksgiving with special food and special people. For what things are you thankful? Talk with a friend about all your gratitude!

2. When Kylie Jean feels nervous, she thinks of Ugly Brother cheering her on. When do you feel nervous? What could you do to feel better the next time you are nervous?

3. What would you do if you won one hundred dollars? Talk about your answer with a friend. Imagine how you could work together!

Be Creative!

1. Kylie Jean sure wanted to help hungry folks. How else could she have helped if there was no cooking competition? Make a list of three ideas, and show it to an adult. Ask if you can try out one of your ideas!

2. Plan a potluck dinner. What dish would you bring? Who could help you cook? Who would you invite? Make a guest list, and write out the ingredients you will need.

3. Draw a picture of a cool apron. Will it be your favorite color? Maybe the apron will have special pockets or a fun image on it!

This is the perfect treat for any Cooking Queen!
Just make sure to ask a grown-up for help.

Love, Kylie Jean

From Momma's Kitchen

Cheesy Macaroni with Ham

YOU NEED:

- 1 package elbow macaroni
- 1/3 cup butter
- 1/2 cup chopped onion
- 2 teaspoons minced garlic
- 2 teaspoons flour
- 3 1/2 cups warmed milk
- 4 cups grated cheddar cheese
- salt and pepper
- 2 cups cubed ham
- 2/3 cup bread crumbs
- 2 teaspoons olive oil

1. Preheat oven to 350°F.

2. Bring a large pot of water to a boil. Add pasta and cook according to package instructions. Drain.

3. Sauté onions in a pot with melted butter for 2 minutes. Add garlic and sauté for another minute. Add flour and stir constantly for 2 minutes. Add milk, stirring constantly until sauce is smooth. Bring to a boil and cook for 1 minute.

4. Remove from heat and add cheese until melted. Then add cubed ham. Season with salt and pepper.

5. Add sauce to cooked pasta. Spoon into buttered casserole dish (9 x 13).

6. Mix bread crumbs with olive oil. Sprinkle over pasta. Bake for 30 minutes.

Yum, yum!

THE FUN DOESN'T STOP HERE!

Discover more at www.capstonekids.com

♥ Videos & Contests

❋ Games & Puzzles

♥ Friends & Favorites

❋ Authors & Illustrators

Find cool websites and more books like this one at www.facthound.com. Just type in the Book ID: **9781479598991** and you're ready to go!